THE ACCIDENTAL ANGLER

BY THE SAME AUTHOR

Somewhere Else

THE ACCIDENTAL ANGLER

Charles Rangeley-Wilson

YELLOW JERSEY PRESS
LONDON

Published by Yellow Jersey Press 2006

7

First published in Great Britain in 2006 by
Yellow Jersey Press

Yellow Jersey Press
Random House, 20 Vauxhall Bridge Road,
London SW1V 2SA

Random House Australia (Pty) Limited
20 Alfred Street, Milsons Point, Sydney,
New South Wales 2061, Australia

Random House New Zealand Limited
18 Poland Road, Glenfield,
Auckland 10, New Zealand

Random House (Pty) Limited
Isle of Houghton, Corner of Boundary Road & Carse O'Gowrie,
Houghton, 2198, South Africa

Random House Publishers India Private Limited
301 World Trade Tower, Hotel Intercontinental Grand Complex,
Barakhamba Lane, New Delhi 110 001, India

The Random House Group Limited Reg. No. 954009
www.randomhouse.co.uk

A CIP catalogue record for this book
is available from the British Library

ISBN 9780224078832 (From Jan 07)
ISBN 0224078836

Papers used by Random House are natural, recyclable products made from wood grown
in sustainable forests. The manufacturing processes conform to the environmental
regulations of the country of origin

Typeset by SX Composing DTP, Rayleigh, Essex
Printed and bound in Great Britain by
Clays Ltd, St Ives plc

To Vicky – my best catch of all

The traveller sees what he sees, the tourist
sees what he has come to see.

G. K. Chesterton

The red light is always on.

Marc Bale, Iceland, 2005

CONTENTS

1   Holy Grayling   1
2   The Breath of a River   10
3   Metal Guru   27
4   The Curse of Shiva   38
5   Non, Ne Pêchez Pas Là!   53
6   My Kingdom Come   71
7   The Year of the Big Fish   90
8   Blame it on the Boogie   109
9   Paradise Found   130
10 Letters Home from a Brazilian
        TV Adventure   149
11 Suburban Sea Trout   167
12 Breakfast in Bhutan   176
13 Wash and Tope   194

    Acknowledgements   205

Holy Grayling

I'VE BEEN MAD ABOUT CATCHING A GIANT GRAYLING ever since a spectral encounter several years ago. I was sneaking up the side of a tree-lined pool in autumn. Sunlight broke through the leaves and shone into the dusky water in patches – like headlight beams on a misty night. I disturbed a shoal of grayling – a dozen fish of between one and two pounds came scattering downriver, turned at the shallow tail, and scattered upstream again. As they did, a grey hull about the size of a large fish kettle swam through the panic-stricken shoal. It cruised between the columns of light, sped up briefly as it passed my leg. I thought it was a salmon. It was that big. But on the second pass it paused long enough across one of the shafts of light for me to see the vermilion dorsal fin in full sail. The fish was massive. Absolutely massive. I think it was over five pounds.

That will sound like a fisherman's tale to those who know grayling, because the biggest ever caught was smaller by some margin. Sean Flanagan's British record from the River Frome in Dorset weighed 4 lb 3 oz, though an unofficial claim from the Itchen exists for a fish 1 oz heavier. The biggest grayling seem to come from the chalk streams. After the Frome and Itchen fish, there are four more claims for fish of around 4 lb – three from the Test at Mottisfont, caught by H. Mordaunt and M. Headlam in 1905, and another from the Chess in 1955, taken by E. Chambers who caught another of 3 lb 13 oz on the same day. The Driffield Canal yielded a 3 lb 14 oz grayling to E. J. Stanton in 1967. Then there was the 3 lb 10 oz fish from the River Allen in 1983 – it held the official record for a while. The important fact is this: nine – only nine – grayling over 3 lb 10 oz. Ever. Only two of which were authenticated. In the context of this list, which I have to confess I read quite often, my Scooby-Doo encounter with the Biggest Grayling That Ever Lived has been a haunting memory.

A couple of years later, fishing the same river for trout in May, I hooked a grayling on a nymph. Grayling can be powerful, especially in December, when the water is cold, and they are steely and fat, and they get sideways across the current. But even then they don't often take you downstream, in that way you see big dogs take anxious old ladies for walks across the park. This one rushed me a hundred yards downriver, under a bridge and out the other side. It settled in a pool until I caught up with it, when it charged upriver again, before snagging itself in a mess of branches.

I'm sure that fish would have broken me if it hadn't swum into the uprooted bush. Finally I was able to gently take hold of its vast bulk before it broke the line. Having touched it I relaxed – it was officially landed. I didn't have a net or scales. But the grayling was ridiculously big. I measured it against my rod; with the tail against the top of the cork, its nose nudged a little beyond the whipping on the top side of the stripper guide: a whisker over twenty-two inches. I like to think that it was a record fish. But I'll never know. Caught out of season it wouldn't have counted anyway. A thought that has proved little compensation for the agonising moment I pushed a potential record back into the stream and set the word potential in stone. By being in the right place at the right time, all record-breakers have bitten on the meaty end of fate's sandwich – either by accident or design. And for a brief moment I was there too. But record-breakers come prepared with nets, scales, and witnesses.

Ronnie fishes this river too, and each year, when the skies clear in the morning, and the leaves curl up coppery at the edges, we call each other and agree it's getting a bit graylingy. We meet by the river, drink coffee and plan a day looking for big ones. It's always leisurely, with no reward for starting early or finishing late. Grayling feed hard in the autumn, but the trick is to find them – they move about like a Bedouin goatherd – and that can take half a day.

Sometimes we don't find any, but we usually end up with a brace of two-pounders, and sometimes one a good deal bigger than that. These are big grayling by any standards, but we are vague about the weight, an absence of precision that, though amateur and gentlemanly, has been bothering us lately. Especially given that others who fish the same stream come prepared with scales, weighing sacks and cameras. They notch up precise bests each winter, and circulate the pictures. The best fish caught by these pros last season was 3 lb 12 oz. A fish that would have held the record a few years ago and which makes it into that list of biggest grayling ever. Ronnie and I spoke about the picture they sent to me.

'It's not that big, Charlie.'

'You're right. We've seen bigger grayling.'

'That's not the biggest, not by a long shot. What are we messing about for, Charlie? We need to get serious. We can't keep putting these enormous fish back without knowing.'

In early September last year, I told Ronnie I'd bought a set of weighing scales. Digital scales. He'd done the same a week before, thinking along the same lines. 'This is it, Ronnie. No messing about for diminutive two-pounders. We're going for the record. We won't even stop to cast unless it looks likely, unless it's really big.'

Reports of large grayling drift in over the autumn. Soon they become impossible to ignore. It might be a good idea to wait for river flows to pick up, but waiting takes too long. Besides it's easy to miss the slot and end up fishing a brown flood in November. The downside of getting there too early is that it is easy to catch a day when the sun is hard and the river is thin. You'll see fish more easily, but they'll be nervous. In the end we just picked a day, and took our chances.

We found a big grayling after only an hour, but the fish slid away into the dark of the pool as soon as I flicked the line back. We waited a while because grayling normally return and feed again, but this one stayed hidden. It was a good day for grayling, but for the skinny river. The relentless wind that so often spoils fishing at this open end of the valley was on hold. The air was warm, the sky broken with billowing white clouds. When the sun burst through we could see everything underwater, including the falling arc of our tiny bead-head flies. We could track them through the water, right down to where the grayling lay. In the meadows by the river a herd of cattle had been left to graze the heavy autumn grass. Some of the cows came over to watch us. They followed us down the riverbank, spooning tongues into snotty noses, rubbing haunches against tired-out fence posts.

Downriver, a grey outline stood out against a shelf of stones on the far side of the stream. It looked like a good grayling – over two pounds – but it wasn't a record. Ronnie took the cast.

'Well, that's our only-cast-at-a-record rule out the window,' he said, lengthening his line over the water.

'Good to practise,' I said.

The grayling moved to Ronnie's first cast, cutting an angle across the gravel, pulling its shadow beside it, until the fish and the shadow turned hard and drifted back with the current to settle. Next time the fly grazed along its flank and the grayling vanished. We waited. Minutes later, the shadow was back, anchored to the bed of the stream. Ronnie changed the fly, and the fish looked at it again. He changed it again, and the same thing happened. 'I'm running out of nymphs to show this beast,' Ronnie said twenty minutes later. Each time we changed fly the shadow would tilt or shimmy. Then suddenly the shadow bolted upriver, the grey fish appearing beside it, and the grey fish took. 'He's got it!' I shouted. But Ronnie had lost sight of the fish in a reflection and didn't strike. The grayling dropped downriver, and didn't even look at another fly.

A shoal of three fish lay under a broken willow upstream. They were nervous at first – as we walked we disturbed a pike which had bolted between them from the reeds under our feet. We'd come to a barrier of Himalayan balsam. Its sticky aroma filled the air, and as we brushed past, ripe seed pods burst, scattering on to the river and under my collar. The fish were lying at the base of a deep hole in the riverbed. I cast under the shadow of the tree upstream, letting the fly drop downriver with the current. Once it rubbed gently along the flank of an inert fish.

I tried lifting as the fly reached the riverbed. When I did this one of the three fish would switch on, twitching or rising slightly in the current. Or it would bolt forward and stop, dropping back while eyeballing the fly, only to resume its inscrutable pose on the riverbed. I changed the fly every so often, until I too had tried nearly every fly in the box: a size 20 hare's ear towed behind a peeping caddis, two tungsten beads on the same cast, Czech nymphs. Ronnie got bored and went back to his fish on the gravel. The biggest fish took once, and spat the fly before I knew he'd eaten it. I swore under my breath, but Ronnie heard me. 'Was it a good one?' The biggest of the three, I told him.

The river was quiet now. Imperceptibly, the day had warmed and fallen asleep. 'Here's the pool where Tony had a big pike on a goldhead,' said Ronnie. 'He said he saw another in there too.' A leaning oak tree stretched out across the pool, which swung in a tight curve through ninety degrees. A deep channel ran from the neck of the pool to a dark hole under the tree. A floating mass of weeds and sticks was hung up on the trailing oak branches. As the sun overhead slowed, so I felt our chances of a good fish slowing too. It may have been a distraction from our grayling hunt, but I decided to try for the pike. I tied on a bright orange fly, six inches long, with flailing tresses of sparkling hair. It looked like a startled Mick Hucknall in drag. The fly swung down and under the branches of the oak tree. Nothing hit it. But as I pulled it back to try again four large and alarmed grayling swam out from under the tree. I stepped aside. I could hear Ronnie pulling line from his reel.

'There's some big fish there, Charlie,' he said. 'Look at that one at the back.' His fly landed opposite and the line bellied down against the current, then straightened. Instantly the rod was alive in his hands, and from under the tree grey flashed against the dark of the pool, lighter and lighter as the grayling lifted in the water, until with a crack like a snapping branch it beat its tail against the surface. It leapt, and re-entered the water clumsily, off balance, and I could see it was the big one. Ronnie pulled it downriver. The line danced up and down as the grayling pulled back.

The fish took off towards the far bank sideways to the current, and suddenly a bow wave cut across towards it from the side. 'There's a pike after it,' Ronnie shouted. Mick Hucknall had woken the entire pool from its stupor. The pike attacked, carving a silver slice through the shallow water. It missed and veered away. Ronnie pulled the grayling towards him protectively, and stamped at the water. The pike turned to strike again, closed in, then bolted for the tree.

'Did he get him?' I asked.

'Yeah,' said Ronnie. 'Look at the marks on his tail. That pike was up for it.'

'He'd never have swallowed him,' I said. 'That is one seriously big grayling.'

We slipped the startled fish into a mesh sack, looped the hook of Ronnie's scales through the handle, and hefted it from the water. 'Holy smoke,' said Ronnie. 'I've got him at three pounds twelve. Three and a half allowing for the bag.' We dropped the grayling back into the water, and switched scales. Mine read the same. 'That's a significant grayling,' I said. 'It isn't a record, but it's only an ounce off the list. The pike's got an ounce of scales in his teeth too. It's a top-ten grayling. It's within an ace of the old Allen record anyway.'

I'd wound Ronnie up. 'That's one for the wall. That's a trophy fish,' he said, hoping I'd agree.

I thought for a moment. I wanted the fish to go back. I always do. 'Four pounds is a trophy,' I said finally. 'He'll recover. Those cuts are small.' Ronnie didn't say anything. He looked a little pale. I took a picture of him holding the fish. Finally he opened the sack, and slid the grayling back into the pool. I knew what he was thinking.

A few weeks ago Ronnie sent me an email with a jpeg attachment of an enormous grayling, stuffed and in a glass case. It was Flanagan's record fish. Ronnie had found it in an antique shop. He says that it will make up for the one that he put back – at least until we find one bigger.

The Breath of a River

FIVE IN THE MORNING, THE SKY AN INKY BLUE BUT lightening to the east over Blackwall and Woolwich, the clang of a bell signals the start of trading at Billingsgate Market. The crisp dawn has a bite to it and I button my coat tight as I cross the car park. A pool of phosphorescent light spills from one corner of the warehouse and encircles a pile of white styrofoam boxes. The cold air suddenly gives way to a warm layer of fishy pong, gone as quickly as it arrived. If I could see smell, the air around the building would be marbled with colours-as-scent grading through fresh fish to forgotten cod head lost behind a hot-water pipe. Men in white coats and hats move urgently in and out of the light, straining trolleys behind them or hefting boxes on their shoulders through the doorway and down the narrow aisles between the fish stalls. 'Scuse me. Mind yer back. Things are too busy just yet. I make myself narrow and look around the stalls.

* * *

Two hundred years ago the River Thames and its tributaries teemed with fish of all kinds – smelt, plaice, flounder, shad, gudgeon, dace, dab, roach, pike, salmon. But most significantly to me because I seem to have a love affair with them – trout and sea trout. One hundred and eighty years ago all those fish had gone. In 1828 Mr Goldham, Clerk of Billingsgate Market, made an address to a Parliamentary Committee which had been set up to investigate the calamity. In the mid eighteenth century there had been four hundred boat-owning fishermen between Deptford and London, he said. Fifty thousand smelt were sent daily to Billingsgate and three thousand Thames salmon were netted each season. As recently as 1810 Mr Goldham had seen ten salmon and three thousand smelt taken in one haul. Now the fishery had been destroyed.

We tend to accept landscape as we find it, imagining that a pavement has always been a pavement, or at least not stopping to think about what came before, about what had to give way. The outrageous change occurs elsewhere – in the Amazon, on the ice caps of the Arctic. It is more surprising than it should be to imagine our landscape before houses and to picture the wilderness that was there for so much longer. I sometimes get gripped by the mad idea that the old Thames is out there as an image travelling at the speed of light through all but the very closest parts of space. If so, the degraded Thames that Mr Goldham described is a tiny and very recent part of that column of light that goes on for ever. I like to imagine it this way, because I like to imagine that things are getting better. Which is why I am standing (mostly in the way of busy fishmongers) in the central aisle of Billingsgate Market at dawn in the last week of September 2005.

Just recently stories have circulated about the idea of a cleaner river. I've heard about bass in the Estuary, sea trout in Deptford Creek, dolphins at Chiswick, the occasional salmon running up through Teddington Lock. A few years ago I heard of a salmon in the outfall of Beddington sewage works.

Salmon in the Thames have grabbed headlines, but I dream of catching a wild trout there instead. Not that I'd mind a salmon or that it wouldn't be significant, but I know they've been stocked, that hundreds of thousands of pounds have been spent trying to regenerate salmon runs. The odd salmon at Teddington Weir or lost in the Wandle is evocative, but perhaps not that surprising. Sea trout in Deptford Creek is a miracle. No one has stocked sea trout. But they roam more than salmon, are more prepared to take a chance on a river that isn't their natal stream, are more able to exploit an ecological niche should one appear.

By seven the market has calmed down. The big orders have been dealt with. Jokes are flying from one fish stall to the other and the intent faces have softened a little. I start to ask around. The first few stallholders shrug and can't help.

'Very rare, aren't they? Like ginger-haired girls. You do see 'em, but they are rare. Why, I don't know.'

I tell him they're rare because the Thames was so polluted, but that I'm hoping to hear it is cleaning up. A wild trout would prove it.

'It's a lovely river. Underestimated now. Years ago, yeah, you'd sit there and catch the flu out the water. You know what I mean? It was diabolical. Terrible. Whether Lee does 'em I don't know. Or you could try Newnes.'

Eventually I find my way to Roger, someone who knows all about Thames fish. In a straw hat, with his glasses at the end of his nose, Roger is busy processing fish orders. I ask if I can pick his brains.

'Not a lot of them, sir. Thames fish? We've got herrings. We've got sprats. We've got Dover sole. This time of the year a tremendous amount of that kind of fish comes out of the Thames Estuary. There's more fish now caught out of the Thames – yeah? What does he want? Thirty-seven and a half pounds of halibut? No problem. The Thames has never been so clean in the last hundred years as it is at this particular time. If you go off Westcliff, which is right on the Estuary, there's even about twelve to fifteen seals, which is a tremendous sign that it is clear, that the fish are good, that there's enough for them to eat. It's just got better and better and better.'

'Do you ever hear about sea trout in the Thames?'
I ask him.

'On the odd occasion.'

Someone shouts 'Liar' from the stall behind.

'We have had them on the odd occasion.'

'Liar.'

'Please ignore my brother. He's just out of a mental institute. We do have them on the odd occasion.'

The sudden-impact death of the Thames in the city was a moment when everything happened at once in one place. But as an image of what took place across Greater London it is incomplete. London's rivers died in waves. Pollution grew in concentric circles creeping very slowly from the Thames to the side streams that run in from north and south like the spokes on a wheel.

Until less than 250 years ago, London was much smaller than Zone 1 on the Underground. The local impact of its pollution was intense – inner London streams were disgusting, and after 1820 so was the Thames. But more significantly the toxic plug London created destroyed the populations of fish that had to swim through it: migratory fish like salmon and sea trout. Even if the streams where they spawned and the sea where they fed were healthy, the cesspit Estuary and city reaches of the tributaries created an impassable barrier.

Later London's rivers died as the city grew to engulf them. A couple – the Lea to the east and the

Colne to the west – still cross a measure of open countryside before they reach the city. Others like the Wandle flow in from the outskirts of London, but are completely urban. Some, like the Fleet and the Tyburn, both of which rise on Hampstead Heath, still flow, but are buried under the streets.

To understand what happened to the city's rivers I need to glimpse into the past, to the London landscape before London engulfed it. William Fitzstephen writing *Vita Sancti Thomae* in 1175 painted a vivid picture of a London impossibly tiny in comparison with today's behemoth, where delightful open countryside was only ever a short stroll from the centre of the city:

On the north side are fields for pasture and a delightful plain of meadowland, interspersed with flowing streams, on which stand mills whose clack is very pleasing to the ear. There are also round London, on the northern side, in the suburbs, excellent springs, the water of which is sweet, clear and salubrious, mid glistening pebbles gliding playfully, amongst which Holy Well, Clerkenwell, and St Clement's Well are of most note and most frequently visited, as well by the scholars from the schools, as by the youth of the city when they go out to take the air in the summer evening.

It's an evocative piece of writing. A word map.

There are no real maps as old as this – we have to wait hundreds of years for the image to catch up. But in 1746 John Rocque drew a map of London and the countryside around it – with such loving detail in depicting hedgerows, lanes, trees and meadows that it and Fitzstephen's ancient text combine to create an almost tactile image of a lost landscape.

The city had grown in the intervening 600 years; Fitzstephen's wells have been absorbed (but only just) by streets and houses. Even so, it is still amazing to the modern eye to see the city end suddenly halfway up Farringdon Street, with Battle Bridge (now King's Cross) a rural hamlet in the valley of the open River Fleet. Other rivers can be traced: the Tyburn flowing south from Hampstead under Buckingham House (not yet a palace) to Westminster; and the West-bourne flowing through Chelsea. Like the Fleet, neither of these rivers can be seen today, and like the Fleet both were spring-fed and must have teemed with trout and other fish.

The story of the Fleet is a crystallisation of what happened to all of London's streams. The Fleet once formed the western boundary of the Roman city; as London expanded it was soon a river running through the centre of the town. It became an open sewer. In 1710 Swift described its awfulness in a ditty in the *Tatler*: 'Sweepings from butchers' stalls, dung, guts and blood / Drown'd puppies, stinking sprats, all drench'd in mud / Dead cats and turnip-tops come tumbling down the flood.'

From time to time the river became so blocked by its tide of dead animals and human excrement that the stream was impassable to boats. Over the centuries several attempts were made to clean it, but it always reverted to the same disgusting state. After the Fire of London Wren designed an elegant canalisation of the lower river, but eventually the pong became just too awful, it was covered over and its official status of sewer was sealed.

Under Blackfriars Bridge an arched tunnel is exposed at low tide. It is all that is left of the estuary of the River Fleet – the estuary that gave the river its common name, a place wide enough to harbour boats. Excepting occasional storm water no flow leaves the tunnel – the river is diverted somewhere below the roundabout between the bridge and New Bridge Street. From Blackfriars looking up the old valley beyond Ludgate Circus, Farringdon Street perfectly traces the line of the old river. I try to imagine what it was like, substituting the taxis for boats, the pavement for riverbank.

Clues are everywhere. Fleet Street dips to Ludgate Circus and rises again after crossing the valley up Ludgate Hill. A few yards upstream is Old Seacoal Lane, where fourteenth-century butchers washed entrails into the river. The Holborn viaduct crosses the old valley. Holborn is one of the four names given to this river – literally the 'bourne in the hole'. Upstream again, beyond the old ford at Cowcross

Street, is Turnmill Street – the river was also called the Turnmill Brook – and a few yards beyond is St Clement's Well, a rural spring in Fitzstephen's day and an echo of the river's fourth name, the River of Wells. Loads of other street names give clues to the course of the river valley – Wells Square, Battle Bridge Road, Water Lane, Spring Place, Pond Street and, in Kentish Town, Angler's Lane. This last street name is the only reference to fishing on the old river that I can find. Not because people didn't fish it much – I'm sure they did – but because the Fleet was so wrecked as a river before anyone bothered to write much about fishing.

At the foot of Angler's Lane, as I cross the road, I catch a familiar smell: the tangy, chewy whiff of treated sewage. Between cars I quickly press my ear to the manhole cover the smell is coming from, and hear the ghost of the river rushing beneath the streets. The Fleet flows on – in pitch darkness, ankle-deep, warm as a bath and full of turds. The only wildlife a few rats.

On Hampstead Heath a few swimmers bob like seals around the men-only pond. And in the pond above them an angler has been fishing for so long the grass has been mown around his tent. I stop to ask if he's had any luck. Nothing so far, he says. He asks me what I'm doing and I tell him that I've followed the Fleet up from Blackfriars Bridge along the course of the lost river to where he's sitting. I say that I'm hoping to find a wild trout somewhere in London. He looks at me. I know I won't find one here, I say, though they must once have been in the Fleet. 'You could try the Lea over at Hackney Marsh,' he says. He's heard some kids caught one there. It's a great place. He's had perch, bream, pike on the Lea. 'Used to be legendary. It still is.' I wish him luck and say if he gets a bite I'll come over to help. 'If I get a bite you'll know about it all right.' As I leave he opens a can of Special Brew. 'Anglers' favourite medicine,' he says.

At the head of this pond a dry stream bed hidden in the undergrowth turns off the steep hill to the east. I fight my way through to it and walk along it a little way. This is the bed of the Fleet. It and the ponds form the only stretch of the old course that hasn't been buried. I'd like to come back here in the winter when the springs are flowing and stand with my feet in the moving water, to feel in touch with a part of the living river.

At the top of the hill I sit down. London is crammed into a bowl in the landscape below me. It all looks so close. The perspective is crushed by the clear light of a late summer evening. The walk that has taken me all day is easy to trace between landmarks, but the lie of the land that would once have been so visible from up here is masked by the topography of buildings.

It seems impossible that I'll ever find a trout in this choppy sea of concrete, but I try to imagine them nuzzling up flooded streets, tracing above ground the rivers that are below it. I follow them and the street names: up the Westbourne past Knightsbridge, Bayswater and Kilburn; the Tyburn along Tachbrook Street and Horseferry Road; the Stamford Brook by Old Acton Wells to Brook Green. But it's impossible. Though a salmon once wedged itself into a water pipe off the Fleet sewer I know I won't find a trout in a buried river. I need to look for places with a little life left in them. They exist. They must do. I've heard of sea trout getting into St Katharine's Dock, or spawning off the back of a car park by the Ravensbourne; in Shepperton weir pool, at the mouth of the Hogsmill. But they are one-off sightings, years and miles apart and never in the same place twice.

Beyond the city I can just make out a rise in the ground, a ridge that forms the edge of the Thames watershed to the south of the main river. To the south-west, from Kingston to Croydon the ridge is made of chalk. At Carshalton along by Ruskin Road and Beddington Sports Ground a river rises in springs and flows north to the Thames near Wandsworth. The Wandle was once so great a river that Royal Preserves were passed to protect its fish. Isaak Walton said that Wandle trout were spotted like tortoises. In 1586 William Camden called it the 'cleare rivulet Wandle, so full of the best trouts'. Though stretches have been canalised and run through culverts, though the chalk springs have mostly been replaced by sewage outfalls, much of it still flows above ground. A friend who travels to work on the Earlsfield–

Waterloo line gets a glimpse of the Wandle every day. He says it looks good, although he's never fished it.

Approaching the Wandle from the west on a different line my train passes over the lowest part of the river. The tide is out, exposing black, oily mud banks littered with tyres, shopping trolleys and what looks like a bedstead. A decrepit barge rots like a whale's carcass, sinking into the goo. I get out at Wandsworth Town and walk down. I find the river and as I lean over the railings I notice a few small fish shimmying back and forth, silhouetted against the white backdrop of a drinks can. It's an encouraging sign but in every other respect the place seems desolate. The air over the water has the strong, acrid smell of effluent. In the nineteenth century a Mr Smee had an ornate garden upstream from here. He wrote about it and the river:

> The Wandle taken as a whole is the perfection of a river; its water is bright as crystal and is purity itself. It does not overflow with rain, nor is it deficient in dry weather. It does not freeze in winter, nor does it become very hot in summer. It has existed through all historic times . . . and it may thus exclaim the words of the poet: 'Men may come and men may go but I go on for ever . . .'

It didn't though. The Industrial Revolution turned

the Wandle from this Arcadian stream to the burning Styx in Hades. By 1805 the Wandle supported twelve calico works, nine flour mills, five snuff mills, three bleaching grounds, five oil mills, two dyeing works, one paper mill, one skinning mill, one logwood mill, one copper mill, one porter brewery: forty-two industries in eight miles of water employing three thousand people.

The river died slowly. A description of the Wandle at Croydon in 1830 refers to the 'nice gravelly bottom for the trout to spawn in' – that part of the river is now buried in a pipe – and trout were caught in it throughout the nineteenth century. It was 1908 before someone described it as 'sage-green and sluggish, a sticky stream soiled by a dozen factories and smelling vilely'. Its last trout – an impressive fish of 5 lb 2 oz – was caught in 1934 and with its passing the river also died. It became so polluted that it once caught fire.

Now the fire is out. Instead mattresses, trolleys and bikes rise out of the depths of the river like some kind of sarcastic coral reef. And under Armoury Way a giant teddy bear anchored in the flow wafts pathetically from side to side. There is something so hopelessly, naffly sad about this teddy. It is neglected, like the river. Unloved when that is the opposite of what is right. Why the hell do people throw rubbish into rivers? They think the river will wash their junk and their shame away. But what's a river going to do with a fridge or a motorbike or a mattress?

The Breath of a River

I walk upstream past the brewery to King George's Park. Here the Wandle looks much better. Shielded on one side by railings, on the other by long back gardens the river through the park is sheltered from the work of the fly-tippers. It is running quickly over clean gravel, and stands of water buttercup break the flow. I even see a few dace picking midges off the surface in the glassy water under the trees. As I leave the park through St John's Drive housing estate two kids spot me in waders, carrying a fishing rod. They come over to chat and follow me all the way to Earlsfield. One of them says he's heard of trout in the river. I want to believe him, but then his friend says trout are like tuna, and that I may even catch a conger eel. While they watch I fish under Earlsfield Bridge – the part of the river my friend told me about – but only catch a small chub.

I carry on upriver, stopping to cast once in a while, or to chat to other fishermen when I see them. Most have heard of trout here, one even says he's caught a couple. But a moment later he says he's only ever seen one. Through Colliers Wood and by the Saver Centre the river looks great. But trout are so sensitive. The river may be treated and clean, but in a storm sewage works overflow, and rainwater washes poison off the roads. Even if sea trout made it up here to spawn it's not certain their offspring would survive for long.

Even so, it is encouraging when at the end of the day I meet Martin who swears the first part has happened already. He fishes here a lot, he tells me, and last year caught a two-pound trout that wasn't stocked. He shows me the picture on his mobile phone. It's a good-looking fish. And it's the first story I have faith in.

I come back the next day to look for it or a fish like it and walk through Mordern Hall Park and upstream to Beddington, Tooting, Hackbridge and Carshalton where the river begins. I look into every part of the stream I can reach. The river is low and clear. It is a good day for looking. I see chub. So many chub. But I don't see any trout.

I think the ghost stories are true. I want to believe them – that trout really are exploring the Thames once again. But without an eternity in which to look, what chance do I have of finding something so spectral in an environment so hostile? I started my journey looking for a shrinking city, receding from its impact on the wilderness that was overwhelmed. Maybe what I have found here is at least the turn of the tide.

This story is about looking for the edge: the edge of destruction, the edge of what is holding on. At its end I am on a train to the suburbs, to the far reaches of the Underground and a different tidal zone of struggle between the sprawling city and what is left of the wild countryside it has grown over. I have travelled to a new landscape of fragrantly named culs-de-sac, of shopping centres, family pubs and football fields. The dull, billowing roar of the M25 washes over everything. Inside its ring of concrete, but on the edge of the Chilterns, the greenery blurs like a colour chart, through shrubberies – cotoneaster, forsythia and cherry – to a handful of wild and forgotten corners of bramble and willow.

But the view is deceptive. This is just another phase in the history of the city and its water, only here the story is underground, and altogether more abstract. Two things seem certain: London needs water, and London will destroy where the water comes from. The destruction was more tangible when the Fleet filled with dead dogs or the Wandle caught fire. Now London's tendrils reach underground to suck water out of the chalk hills that surround it. A few years ago a Chiltern stream called the Misbourne dried up from source to mouth – twenty miles of riverbed sacrificed to a fulsome flush. Two hundred years ago the Thames salmon run was finished off by what came out of London's new toilets. Today the threat is what goes into the cistern.

I'm within yards of the M25. Behind me London sits like a leech on the landscape. All day I've been searching for an accident of suburban evolution: a lost river that isn't in a park, that isn't an urban amenity, that isn't in a pipe, that is still flowing – and the trout that I hoped would give it life. But ankle-deep in an emaciated stream what I've been searching for suddenly seems beyond reach. The river feels washed out. It is hardly flowing. I flick a roll-cast upstream ahead of me, aiming it at nothing in particular. The fly disappears in a splash and a tiny brown trout tumbles towards me, flicking across the surface, fizzing like a firework.

God at His best. The breath of a river. This is the edge.

Metal Guru

SEPTEMBER HAD NEARLY PASSED WHEN I CALLED THIS time round. We'd been busy and nothing was even on the table. My plan was simple. Richard liked the idea and said he'd call Tony – 'Tony'll get us into a fish if anyone can.'

A day later – Friday now – Tony was on the phone, saying everything was set. Rain was already falling and was due to fall harder over the weekend. We'd meet on Monday at Ecclefechan, just over the border. Tony's good pal George had a few beats on the Annan, which would fish well. George was ready for a boarding party. 'He'll sort us out,' said Tony. 'It's official, we can get excited about this one.'

Every other autumn Richard and I plan some expedition after salmon, though we rarely catch them. Hoping one day we'll step into our idea of the perfect salmon river – cheap, undiscovered, full of fish – we've been to Ireland, Devon, Wales and Scotland, endured half a dozen chintzy, damp bedrooms and flogged miles of empty water for little more than the odd kipper. We've come to the point that I doubt either of us really believes in it any more. But then the memory of the last disastrous trip wears thin, we suspend our cynicism, make our plans, and chase them to their inevitable conclusion.

We got our rain – too much of it. I stopped in Appleby on the way and took a despairing look at the Eden, which ran dark and high under the bridge in the centre of town. I found Richard on the mobile and told him the Eden was like a molten Mars bar. I don't think he heard me. He was more animated about being driven up the M6 in a roll-up haze. 'If I could read the signposts I'd tell you where we are. Oh God! Tony's rolling another.' I pressed my urgent message home. 'Hang on. I'll see what Tony thinks.' Tony's gravel voice drawled calmly in the background. 'It's all right, Chuck. Tony says relax. It will be fine. The Annan will be just perfect.'

But the next morning, as we drove from Ecclefechan to Hoddom Bridge and the clouds lifted, peeling away from the glistening landscape, the river ran through the trough of the valley to our right, a dark strip through the green, shining fields.

'Oh hell, Chuck, it's a ribbon of caramel porridge. We got a bloody spate all right.'

The lane steepened under a canopy of beech trees, turning sharp right on to Hoddom Bridge. The storm had shaken a thick layer of leaves on to the road, and as we pulled in, the lorry behind swung past pumping its air brakes and locking wheels. The anglers on the bridge pressed themselves against the parapet to let it through and then turned back to the river. They crossed from one side to the other and we walked over to join them. The water was coppery and thick, and above the near arch it lapped the low branch of an alder tree which snapped back and forth, bowing and giving in the current. We continued with the ritual examination, as though the water might clear as we watched it or some other detail not yet noticed might swell to deny the obvious – that the river was far too high for fly fishing, that it was time for spinners and worms.

Most of my early trout fishing was done like this in Ireland, and I caught my first salmon with a worm on a tributary of a rather posh Scottish river – I had been allowed to play there in the evening and I marked the fish in the hotel book as having fallen to an Uzumbulu fly. So I've never had a great problem with salmon purism: I'll catch the feckers how I can, though obviously it's more fun on a fly rod. Richard was curling his nose up though, and I knew it. Tony too. He took a last look at the water and said he'd get bored too quickly using a spinner so he was off to do a little work on the cottage he was selling. Richard briefly looked like he might want to join him.

'Show me the river and I'll pull some tin through it,' I said.

George had stopped up at the ornate gateway by the bridge in a big, black off-roader. He took us upstream down a slippery terrace of fields to an inside bend where the Annan pushed wildly, dragging at the low branches of the trees opposite so that they moved up and down in the water like oars. We were on the part of the river that George keeps for himself and his mates. The anglers we'd seen on the bridge were fishing his other beats on day tickets. As we set up, the one thing we were sure about was that the flood must have brought fish up from the Firth into the river. But we all doubted they'd see far enough through the smoky water to notice our lures. George tied on a bright silver spoon and as he walked up the bank his two Labs spun crazily around him, jumping up and trying to eat it, hooks and all.

Richard yawned after his sixth cast. I moved down the pool slowly, trying to fish methodically, to cover each lie. After a few minutes George was back and pulling a pack of ciggies out of his coat. Richard, who doesn't smoke except when he's fishing with absolutely no hope of catching anything and when the ciggies belong to someone else, lit up keenly. The two of them fell into a long chat. The morning ticked away. I was on my third run down the pool while their voices droned softly behind me and the river lapped darkly at my feet, when a gigantic salmon the colour of tinfoil coated in treacle turned at the lure. The water surface stirred moments after it had vanished back into the darkness. I looked at the others and moved my mouth – though no words came out. I tried again.

'A fish. A fish turned! Just now. Right here, under me. A bloody great big salmon!'

Richard and George stopped talking for a moment while I backed up and tried to cover the spot again. But the fish stayed hidden and after a few minutes it was as if nothing had happened. I worked over the spot for a fourth time, and then down to the end of the pool for the sake of thoroughness. The others had stopped paying attention and were chatting again when a new fish hit my lure. It was twenty yards below me and close to where the river spilled fast over hidden rocks. The fish cut back and forth levering against the press of water, turned and nearly got away. I ran alongside and pulled, trying to get it to the edge. Richard had by now woken up to the fact that there really were fish about and was already below me ready to scoop it out of the water. But the salmon had taken me out of the pool into the riffle below and was close to some really fast water, turning sideways in the current and gathering steam. I was beginning to doubt I'd see the fish again, when it scythed back towards the still water and I quickly skimmed it into the bank. Richard grabbed the tail, and threw it up the slope – a bright cock-fish straight off the tide. I quickly pinned it to the bank in case it rolled back. I don't think we looked dignified and I don't suppose, given that George owned the beat, we hid our amazement well enough. But then George hadn't been salmon fishing with us before.

'Bloody hell. We've actually caught one,' said Richard.

That evening, back at the hotel in Ecclefechan we heard a few other fish had come off the river that day, in spite of the flow. One of the anglers in the bar had his biggest ever salmon at fourteen pounds, regretting only that it fell to a spinner. The river was fining down, the men said. They'd use a fly as soon as they could. And suddenly there was this unwritten sense in which none of the fish counted.

'Yup, you can't beat a fly,' said the man's friend. We nodded. 'But, you know, you catch them how you can. We'll use a fly right enough. Soon as the river clears.'

'Well, it's clearing now, I bet,' I said.

'Let's hope so!'

We met at Hoddom again the following morning and as we walked on to the bridge to have a look at the water level someone was already bending into a fish in the run downstream. I ran down to speak to the angler. He was puffing hard trying to steer the fish towards his friend's net, so I let him get it in before asking what he'd caught it on. 'Flying Condom,' he said looking up. Then he shrugged, half apologetically. I went back to the others. When I told them, Tony decided to do a few more things on his house and Richard groaned. We went back to the same beat, and I caught two more salmon on my bright blue lure.

After a decade of trying, this ought to have looked like success. Richard did his best to be excited: we even took a trip into town to find a copy of the sucessful lure for him to use. But the local shop didn't stock it and that killed the attempt. We dawdled over lunch, took a half-hearted look at the river in the afternoon. I made few casts. Richard fired himself up with manufactured enthusiasm and borrowed my rod. But the glucose hit didn't last for long. He hooked a fish on it, and couldn't have looked less excited winching it in. It had become waiting-room fishing. We needed the river to clear.

We met up with Tony and George in the pub that night. Tony was coming round to the idea of fishing the next day. The river might have dropped enough for the fly by then. I could tell he was serious because while we drank he rang his mate Ian encouraging him to join us. And the jungle drums must have beaten hard because not long after that Tony's mobile vibrated itself across the varnished table.

'Hello? . . . Hello, Metal Mickey! How's it going? . . . Yes. It's looking pretty good. Clearing nicely and there are a few fish about . . . You thinking of coming up?'

Richard was feeling more upbeat and for a while I allowed myself to be seduced by their purism. Taking a salmon on a fly *is* better, *is* more artful, more difficult. Isn't it?

I was just saying something about how I really wanted to catch one of these fresh fish on a fly when

Tony put his phone down and said: 'Well, don't fish upstream of Mickey then.'

The next day I lost my touch. And I was upstream of Mickey. His white van was perched on a hill above a pool called the Dilholm, his favourite spot. I tried a too adventurous reach under thick trees, lost my killing Rapala on a rock, and the day went quickly downhill. At lunch Richard returned from downriver with the news that Mickey had caught five on a three-inch silver Toby spinner. The river was clearing, but no one had caught anything with the fly. Mid-afternoon Tony came up the bank in his Aussie hat, fly rod hung at his side like a six-shooter, and said that Mickey had caught another four.

Nine fish in a day? Who does that? I picked up my spinning rod and went down to meet this metal guru. Away downriver I could see a figure under a terrace of tall trees. The figure seemed to be wrestling with something. It couldn't be another salmon. The path downstream peeled away from the river, rising above the cliff of beech trees. I walked through the wood at the top of the slope, trying to glimpse the river, to guess where Mickey was standing. Finally I found a switchback path that dropped down the steep bank. I called out. A voice answered from beyond the trees. By the time I found Mickey the huge fish was at his side.

'He got round the tree and pegged it by the time I got him in. Had to kill him. Still, it's a fresh fish. Shame you didn't get here sooner.'

'Is that your tenth?' I asked, without hiding my disbelief.

Metal looked suprised. He half closed his water-blue eyes, and counted back. 'Well, I suppose it is, now I think about it.'

I wondered how anyone could catch ten salmon in a day in Scotland and not think about it. I'd write an opera about it. I asked if he wouldn't mind showing me what he was doing that I wasn't.

'Up and across,' he said. 'Bring it back as slow as you like.' Mickey snuck back under the trees and fired his silver lure under the low branches towards a narrow gap in the debris on the far bank. It was an unbelievable cast. I went upriver and found an open patch of ground to try the technique. Mickey seemed to give the lure a supercharged flick, allowing him to send it through gaps in trees with the trajectory and accuracy of an arrow. He was fishing places no one else dared to. I tried to copy him and got the bird's nest from hell for it. As I plodded up the bank laying out yards of coiled nylon, and plodded back down to my reel with the laid-out nylon caught on my boot, Mickey hooked another fish. It ambushed him from under a tree where it should have been impossible to get a lure. There was nothing, I thought, nothing at all less artful about what Mickey was doing. It was just more effective.

'Sometimes they hook themselves,' he shouted up at me, shrugging like he couldn't quite help it.

I pulled hard at the Gordian knot as Metal hooked

the next fish – only a sea trout – and garrotted my finger half off when he hooked the one after that. By the time I had finished untangling my line it was dark and Metal had just returned his fourteenth fish of the day. The man was an otter.

I don't know why but that evening after a few pints I became more not less keen to finally catch my fish on a fly, to tag some kind of ethical triumph to the last morning of our autumn salmon trip. I had just seen how spinning can be as artful as you make it, but in the morning I left my spinning rod behind. Perhaps Mickey had made it look too easy. Perhaps fly fishing had become a haven from failure.

We got up early, but there was already a bright fish on the bank by George's car when we arrived at the corner pool. Richard went to wrestle his rod out of the car in a hurry. The day seemed to have acquired some urgency. We had to leave after lunch and at some stage Metal would arrive downstream of us at the Dilholm, something we reckoned would reduce our chances by half. The fly hooked the back seat as he pulled the rod out backwards. 'Oh hell, they hook everything but fish,' said Richard, despairing before he'd started. But the river was clear now, and two foot down from the height of the deluge. The fish in the corner pool were back on the far side under trees. Once in a while a salmon would splash where the riffle curled under the first branches.

The take of a salmon on a fly seems such an easy

event. The line straightens and there it is spinning on the end of the line – a random intersection between a feather and a fish that always feels as though it ought to occur more often. The sun sliced in at an October angle, cutting a soft yellow line between shadow and light across the river. Two strands of twinkle at the tail of my fly caught the light, and briefly glistened as the fly pulled round out of the shadow. A pulse of coppery silver turned up through the flow, my line straightened and there was my fly-caught salmon, lice on the tail, polished bright by the sea.

The Curse of Shiva

The Attributes of the Good Angler: the patience of Job; the eye and observance of the eagle; the perseverance of the termite; the hands of the artificer; the touch of a musician; the temper of a saint; and, above all, an insatiable ambition to learn.

Circumventing the Mahseer, *A. St J. Macdonald*

FINALLY IN BED AND EXHAUSTED, I COULDN'T SLEEP. I could hear the river, although we hadn't seen it yet, rushing over rocks at the base of the slope. The stars were dense and clear, and a cooling breeze blew through the open sides of the hut. I lay on the hard mattress, trying to picture the river out there in the dark, imagining its giant mahseer resting on vortices of foaming water and slowly, slowly, I drifted away.

I slept fitfully in those last few hours before dawn, and my dreams were pretty weird. Over our midnight drink Saad had told us the valley turned into a furnace by day, and this statement must have crept into my subconscious. I woke briefly to see the dawn sky glowing to the east, a fiery band above which faded the endless blue of night, the stars still visible. Smoke from the campfire drifted through my tent. Then I floated in and out of sleep, and suspended like this I dreamt of the sun as a fierce and merciless god, burning up the land. I heard the roar of an army on horses. The thumping hoof-fall grew louder and receded over and over again, before the first rays broke through the trees along the ridge.

I lay pinned to the bed by my own exhaustion while my mind raced away with these strange images, until, provoked by the building heat, I forced myself to sit up. The darkness was quickly draining from the gorge, and the Kaveri River came slowly into focus, a shiver of white merging into sandbanks and rocks, rapids and oily pools. And now that I could see it, the all-enveloping white noise of the water receded as the day brightened.

The river had fetched us here. It is always a river. There is a pause, when the abstract noun takes form and assumes a wet and musty reality, when you see the river for the first time, having only imagined it and said its name a few times. We travel for that moment.

I looked around. The camp was perched on the side of a slope, a collection of tree huts. Mine was anchored to the rocks along one side, but suspended around a tree at the outer edge, from where the slope fell away twenty feet or more. The floor was made of bamboo poles strung together, the roof of bamboo poles split in half, their leaves still attached. Oil had leaked from a lantern on the table. It was full of dead ants. I looked sideways. Ronnie was still asleep. The camp dog was under Ronnie's bed. She beat her tail on the floor a few times, turned and lay back down.

A pair of brain-fever birds had been at it since dawn. Their rising and falling calls had been joined by all sorts of chirrups, whistles, grunts and caws. Mumbled voices and coughing came from a hut higher up the slope behind me. Outside it two guides were stirring a pot over a fire. Sitting up in bed, I watched another guide walk slowly down the hill and across an apron of rocks to start a generator which pumped water to a tank above the camp. Rod and Nick were thumping around in the next hut along. It was time to get up.

The city stretches endlessly. Traffic pulses and throbs, swerves and beeps, like some colony organism, like ants, or like blood in a body. Isolated modern buildings, polished and expensive, soon give way to a reef of single-storey blocks and shacks stretching for miles, before they peter out amid irrigated fields of rice and sugar cane. Nothing is finished. The road alternates randomly from smooth and modern to fractured, ancient tarmac. A geometry of half-built structures, piles of sand, piles of rock scattered along the roadside or in the scrub, awaiting some forgotten purpose. Speeding quickly in the dark across open country, sweeping in broad curves between rolling mounds of rock. Avenues of banyan trees, striped in red and white, flashing past in the headlights.

I saw a picture once – I've forgotten where exactly – a picture that started this journey years before I got on the plane. I can remember the image clearly: a tumultuous pool as backdrop, milky, swirling water, and someone standing in the river cradling an enormous fish, a fish so big that it was outside anything I had experienced. At the time I was catching six-inch trout in County Kerry on a spinner, the same way as this behemoth had been caught in India. That idea particularly took hold of me: the game fish of the Raj. In every other way, though, I might as well have been looking at a fish from the moon. But the picture burnt into my memory – the scales like armour, the fins like the wings on a jet fighter, the small ink-black and menacing eye – and the memory made this outlandish fish familiar. I read more here and there: *The Rod in India*, *Circumventing the Mahseer*, *Somewhere Down the Crazy River*. Gradually, the unreachable idea became a possibility and the possibility became a compulsion. A compulsion that brought me here to my first morning on the banks of the Kaveri River.

Saad Bin Jung, grandson of the Maharaja of Bhopal, made a century against the West Indies on his First Class debut before the mahseer bug got him too. Along with an unlucky illness it took him away from a life in cricket. Saad took the lease on this stretch of the Kaveri and now dedicates himself to the conservation of the mahseer, a fish that is threatened from all sides. Two enormous pipes divert much of the Kaveri's flow from some way upriver to feed the booming infotech centre of Bangalore. Saad told us over breakfast that the river was low and warm and that therefore the fishing was difficult.

Jeremy, the only other guest left in camp, had been here for two weeks and was having a tough time of it. Stuck in a bad patch he'd had nothing for several days, and like Hemingway's old man was 'salao'. None of us knew what to expect. I don't suppose anything could have dented our enthusiasm.

We began the day at Crocodile Rock. Ronnie and I had Suhban as guide. Suhban's name had woven itself through most of the stuff I had read about mahseer in the lead-up to this trip. Suhban was a legend. He took us upstream to the top of a long, greasily silent pool. He wore flip-flops and shorts, a cap with a feather in it, and a loose T-shirt. He carried his bait in a plastic bag, and coughed terribly with the strain of climbing the vast boulders along the river edge. We followed him without speaking.

By nine the sun had cracked into every cool hollow on the valley floor. Suhban sat for a moment and rolled a cigarette. He smiled at me, then clamping the cigarette in his lips pulled out of the bag a large dark brown lump that looked like an elephant turd – the ragi paste the guides had been cooking over the pot at dawn. Suhban kneaded it into a ball. He laid it on a rock, then pulled at my reel until the line hung loose enough to work with. He threaded a hollowed plastic core of electrical wire on to the line and wrapped a thin strip of roofing lead around the plastic. This he pinched tight with pliers. He tied on a large hook, and moulded the bait on to it.

I stood watching with sweat dripping over my forehead and down my back. Suhban checked the multiplier drag, adjusting the star ratchet until line could be pulled only with some effort, then swung the bait out into midstream where he let it settle on the riverbed. He handed me the rod, gestured for me to sit and wordlessly repeated the process for Ronnie. My spinning rod had been leant against a rock, and clearly I wasn't to use it. I felt a little flat that we were bait fishing so soon.

I found a shady hollow in the rocks, but before long my shade had gone, and the day began to boil. I laid down my rod for a bit and shifted uneasily, trying to find somewhere comfortable. It was difficult to sit still on the hot rocks. They burnt and numbed my arse no matter how I sat. But Suhban scowled at the sight of the unattended rod, and I picked it up again quickly. The bait stayed in place and the sun bore down. I was finding it hard to stay awake now, and for a while I must have nodded off with my chin on my fist.

I'm jolted awake by a sudden pull on the end of the line. The rod stabs down with surprising violence, I lift it into a feeble strike as quickly as I can but the fish is gone. Suhban coughs from the shadow of a boulder. I look up and smile, but he doesn't smile back.

By midday the forest is exhausted under the blow-torch heat. Only a few birds sing. A fly buzzes near my head. The rushing sound of the rapid at the head of Crocodile drifts down to me on the breeze and dies at my feet.

About an hour later my line began to lift and drop, and then came the same sudden pull. I stood and set the hook. For a few moments the fish pulled hard, ripping nylon off the reel. I turned to Suhban grinning keenly, thinking that only a good fish could have moved such a stubborn drag. But Suhban walked slowly to the river's edge without enthusiasm. He smiled though and gestured that I should just wind it in. The fish weighed only eight pounds. But it was my first mahseer. I asked Suhban to hold it for a picture, but he looked awkward and I could tell he thought it rather too small to bother with.

That evening Rod caught a better fish. It had been quiet and stupefying all day – Ronnie and I had fished upriver without a further strike, and returned feeling subdued. Suddenly Nick rushed into camp looking for a camera. It was nearly dark. He muttered something about a fish and we stumbled after him across the rocks to the beach below the camp rapid where Rod was standing waist-deep in the river surrounded by three guides, his shirt wet through, as though he had just been baptised. On a stringer in the shallows was a golden mahseer of about thirty pounds. One of the guides shone his torch, but the narrow beam could not take in the whole fish. The circle of light moved up and down this incredible creature, flashing off scales the size of saucers. This was fishing different from anything I had ever done before. This was like hunting tigers.

And slowly, after two fruitless days, the significance of the fish I missed on the first morning sank in. Each strike was hard won and followed hours of inactivity under a sweltering sun, shifting from one buttock to the next on rocks that were boiling hot and uncomfortable.

* * *

The Mahseer's First Rush – I came to the conclusion that though he might not make so long a fight of it as a salmon, he yet made a more difficult one, because his attack was more impetuously vehement, his first rush more violent, all his energies being concentrated in making it effective, though his efforts were, and from that cause, could not be, sustained so long.

The Rod in India, *Henry Sullivan Thomas*

Suhban's brother Bashir took Rod and me to the far end of Kapigowdar, the long, musty pool downstream of the camp, where water drains through a narrow gap in the rocks and quickens down a narrow chute that curls and disappears. It was a long cast to land the bait just ahead of the chute where the fish lay. Bashir threw the first line, and handed me the rod when the bait had settled.

Used to hours of inactivity I took my time, letting my attention wander for a moment to pick out the most obviously buttock-shaped rock. As I turned my head the rod was pulled so hard I nearly lost it. Bashir tried to grab the reel to tighten the drag, and I tried to lift the rod to strike. Somewhere in the middle of all this the fish, which had felt briefly like a runaway quarry truck, got clean away. The line fell limp across the surface of the water, which hadn't even stirred. Bashir shrugged his shoulders. I looked at the river imagining the size of that fish, and the days I'd have to wait for another chance.

Rod was good enough to keep quiet. But hours later, as the squid-ink dark leached up the eastern sky, and the far edge of the pool began to fade from sight, and nothing at all else had happened, he said, 'Well, I reckon you just about wrecked the pool with that missed fish of yours.'

We sat there for a second, thinking about packing in, when a fish hit Rod's bait. The nylon unpeeled from his reel with the sound of frying eggs. Rod braced his feet against the rocks and held on. The water heaved over the green rocks and a bow wave scythed downriver, caught the current, accelerated and was gone. The heavy nylon sang briefly with the strain, and broke. In the few seconds that follow a disaster like that I think we have the briefest hope that time can run backwards and give us a second chance. We watched the water dumbly like this as though we were waiting for the fish to come back.

We were packing up and both feeling a bit sick when one of the small boys from camp approached us and chattered away with Bashir, who turned to us to explain that one of our friends downriver had caught a good fish, and that we must go to see it. We hadn't the appetite. We tried to suggest we shouldn't bother. The little boy stood uneasily, and Bashir insisted.

The fish was at Crocodile Rock, but it was dark before we got there. Caught in a confused jumble of torchlight, Nick was waist-deep in the river cradling the biggest freshwater fish I had ever seen, while the rest of the party stood chatting on the riverbank. It was the first fish of any kind Nick had ever caught. He grinned in the stroboscope of flashguns. The mahseer – with its erect dorsal fin like a standard in the wind, its armour-plated head out of which peered two small, black eyes, and a chain mail of silver and bronze scales – had the look of some oriental knight ready for battle. Nick is tall, but the fish made him look small.

I asked Saad how heavy it was.

'About sixty pounds, we think.'

Nick didn't even have to move to get a beer from the cooler that evening. He sat in the high chair saying if anyone wanted tips from the expert they should just let him know, adding casually that he'd probably give up fishing when he got home.

Jeremy was here on his annual fishing trip and had ended his sixth day without a strike. From an Air-Stream caravan in the West Country he made money however he could, saving up for a month away every year trophy-hunting around the world. He looked low, but said he'd done too much fishing to think that this was anything other than a bad streak. He was just going to fish his way out of it. On the way to bed he mentioned it was his birthday.

'Well, there you go,' I said. 'You'll get one in the morning. We both will.'

* * *

Mahseer have disappeared from our rivers for many reasons: constant dynamiting of the pools – sometimes more than 35 explosions are heard in a morning; excessive netting with nylon nets – fish do not have a chance; new dams have submerged miles of fast water where mahseer spawn; introduction of new species.

From a letter by DeWet Van Ingen,
6 August 1977*

Saad was keen for Jeremy to get a fish. At dawn he

---

*DeWet Van Ingen held the record for the biggest mahseer ever taken on a rod and line – a fish weighing 120 pounds caught from the Upper Kaveri in 1946.

sent Rafik to catch some crabs, a mahseer delicacy, and he packed him off with Suhban to stake out Crocodile Rock. I was getting fidgety with this buttock boiling and asked if I couldn't fish some of the white water with a spinner. Saad said he'd keep me company, but when my plan was explained to Suhban he shrugged and looked at my expectant spinning rig, and shrugged again.

Between each of the smooth and chapel-quiet pools the Kaveri River thundered. I had to climb over steep black boulders, picking my way along ledges, sliding across polished slopes of rock to the river. The water pressed under and around these gigantic rocks, in one pool boiling up from beneath a block of stone fifty feet high. I saw daylight shine green through the water from the far side. I burnt my hands as I climbed. It felt great to be on the move again.

I sat with Saad on the ledge at Ajibora while he held a crab as bait in the fast water.

'You know,' he said, 'this river will always humble you as an angler. If you come here expecting to catch a fifty-, sixty-pound mahseer, with the wrong attitude, the river will disappoint you. But if you come here hoping to see one, to cradle one that maybe you, maybe someone else has caught, that's the right way.'

He wasn't talking to me about me, but he might as well have been. He was talking about the roller-coaster ride that eventually gives way to an acceptance of fate, of what the river will give you. But it isn't always easy to be so philosophical. Not after so long.

When I caught up with the others at lunchtime I was told that Ronnie had taken a mahseer of forty-four pounds, and Rod one of forty pounds. I nodded towards Jeremy, and Ronnie shook his head. Jeremy had moved his crab halfway through the morning, and had snagged it on a rock. There had been shouting.

*   *   *

Shiva as Great Lord Mahadeva is the creator who restores what as Mahakala he destroys.

Lord Shiva's birthday followed Jeremy's and dawned like an iron foundry. At breakfast Saad told us that we could fish at Jenukal – the honey rock. Jeremy sat up.

'That's where they are. That's not been touched for days. That's where the fish are. I know it.'

Jenukal lies in a steep canyon below Mekhedaatu, the goat's leap, a sacred spot where youngsters from Bangalore come to picnic and party. It would be busy today, a public holiday. We had to cross the river in a coracle to get to the fishing ledges on the far side, and already there was a fire upstream, and people were leaping across the rocks, shouting loudly. Saad said that once in a while someone would jump off the ledge in drunken exuberance. Their bodies would wash up at the tail of Jenukal. Rafik looked up anxiously as he paddled us across. The rock face towered high above us.

Rod sat on the lower ledge with Jeremy and Suhban, while Nick and I climbed further upstream with Rafik. We settled on a glass-smooth rock ledge forty feet above the water. It was an oven from the start. We had no shade. We were sheltered from the breeze by hot, black rocks, and by nine o'clock I was a burning heretic. Nick lay down, and I picked up a book, balancing it open with my feet while I held on to the rod. More revellers showed up, and lit another fire. A gang of biker boys revved up and down the jungle track. I watched a large family of monkeys playing – scruffy, curious monkeys that came close, twitched their eyebrows and scurried away again. One, with a scarred nose, came within a few feet of me and sat there baring his teeth and scratching his arse. I went back to the river, but moments later heard a squeal. He had one of his clan in a doggy position and watched me watching him, chuffed as John Holmes with shades on.

Suddenly Jeremy was into a fish. I heard his reel first, giving line against the ratchet. Suhban stood up and was quickly by his side. I could see the bend in the rod. The rest of us took our baits out of the water and watched in silence. The line cut a small wake across the still pool, and the mahseer swam up and down, deep under the surface. When it finally tired and came to the top, Suhban nodded and Rod shouted back that it was a big one. Suhban led Jeremy down the steep rocks to the ledge by the water. Jeremy, transfixed by the fish, said nothing. The mahseer surged again, diving beyond the point of rocks below us, but Jeremy won back the line he'd lost. Soon after, the fish lay on its side at Suhban's feet, and he threaded a stringer of soft rope through its mouth and gills. Rafik led the fish around the ledge so that we could photograph it where Jeremy was able to stand in the river. I took the pictures on Jeremy's camera. I noticed he was shaking.

'How big, Suhban?' I asked.

Suhban smiled and shook his hand, palm down.

'About forty-five maybe.'

'Well, that's it, Jeremy. Shiva has lifted the curse.'

We fished on. Nick got the next strike and a mahseer of thirty pounds. Jeremy had two more strikes, one like an express train, and then he caught a second big fish.

I watched the monkeys.

Non, Ne Pêchez Pas Là!

A POD OF GRAYLING IS GATHERED TIGHTLY TOGETHER on the bed of the stream in a deep pool below a tree stump, shifting in the washing current like interlocking braids of rope pushed open and pulled tight again. The tree's roots bump out into the stream and send a vortex licking the concrete wall below, along the terrace of a house. From the shallow above, strings of ochre weed rise up and lie flat on the surface. A wooden punt tethered to the bank hangs at an angle, half submerged. I have no idea what time it is. In the sunlit parts of the stream I remember the heat, but feel the day is unfolding elsewhere. I look up and I don't know where I am. We have moved way downriver into the town.

I'm giving Cyril's technique my best shot, trying to hammer the nymph in, but it merely arcs up behind and drops in front like a tethered ball. Once in a while I get one cast to drop at the right speed, the tiny nymph sucking bubbles in behind it, but when I do the fly is never on target. It's like trying to steer a brick on the end of a rubber band. I try again and again. Cyril is getting impatient. Suddenly a cast lands where it should. The fly drops towards the riverbed and the fish. I'm tracking the fly with the rod tip, but lose sight of it and move the rod too slowly. '*Non*.' Cyril grabs my arm and speeds it up, pushing it high and swinging on a downstream arc. He lets go of me as the fly tickles past the grayling. But the grayling ignores it. '*Animation*, Charles! *Animation*!' Cyril holds his arm in the air and gestures a trembling lift of the rod. I try again. I lift the fly, too early, too late. I slow it down. I drag it onwards or sideways. We move from one grayling to the next, showing each fish only a few casts, moving slowly downstream. There are fish in every pool and dip in the riverbed, under every bush. A fish nods at the fly. Cyril shouts, '*Oui*,' and I miss it. *Merde*. I don't tell him I was looking in the wrong place. 'Charles!' He looks at me, disgusted. I shrug, as if to say it's only fishing after all. '*La pêche est un sport extrême*,' he reminds me. '*C'est difficile. C'est très, très difficile.*' He asks me how long I have been fishing. I think for a moment and reply '*Vingt-cinq ans*.' Cyril raises his eyes, and makes the kind of noise I imagine a grayling might make ejecting a fly. This shaven-legged, camo-fetishist Frenchie is wondering whether I'm up to it! I can't believe it. The bloody grayling can't be that difficult.

The stream flowed on through the outskirts of L'Isle sur la Sorgue, past back gardens, nuzzling along

Ronnie with the big grayling

The Thames

An urban trout

...chard fishing
...e Annan

The salmon we'd
been waiting for

DeWet Van Ingen's record mahseer in Mysore Museum

FACING PAGE
Rod playing a mahseer

Nick's sixty-pound mahseer

Mahseer in the Kaveri River at the foot of Ramanthpura Temple

The Sorgue at Fontaine de Vaucluse

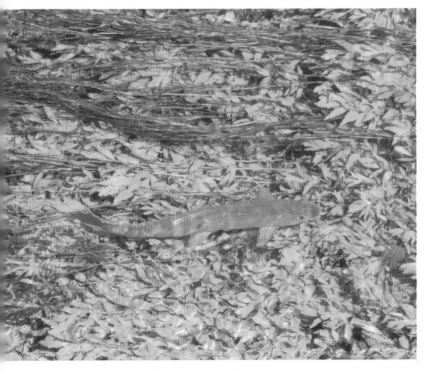

A Sorgue grayling

Cyril doing a King Kong

jetties and concrete pilings, under fig trees. The water deepened. Soon we were wading up to our chests, the frigid water lapping at my shirt, creeping up to my ribcage. We had come to the base of the island. The two streams rejoined. Cyril wanted to get around to track back up the other channel. I waited for him to show me the way. Eventually he put his rod sideways across his mouth, climbed on to the ivy clinging to the sheer bank and shimmied round like King Kong on the side of a skyscraper. He winked, the fly rod still in his mouth. I followed. The emerald pool dropped deeply away below us. We could go no further. We were stuck. Above us was a white fence and the back lawn of a house. Cyril heaved himself up and peered over the edge. He said there was a big dog that lived there. He couldn't see the dog. He thought the old lady, its owner, was out at the market. Quick! he said and with a scramble he was up the wall and in the garden. He crouched for a moment, alert, and then he was gone. I waited.

A whispered shout came from the far side of the garden. He was calling me to follow him. I climbed up, stepping on a branch which broke with a loud crack just as I heaved myself into a pile on the lawn. A dog barked. I looked up. Cyril was crouched behind a pile of logs. The side door of the house opened slowly. Cyril was beckoning me urgently. I jumped up and ran after him, past the side door and on, not looking or waiting for anything. The old lady was not out. She squealed something loud and hysterical as we ran over her terrace. I heard the dog scrabbling for grip. Cyril vaulted the wall and landed somewhere beyond, out of sight. The dog was behind me now. I wasn't waiting to get bitten. I jumped the wall and grabbed at the fronds of ivy hanging off a branch to slow my fall. I entered the water arse first, still clutching at the ivy, but somehow I righted myself to a standstill, waist-deep. '*Charles,*' cried Cyril, '*La pêche est un sport extrême. N'est-ce pas?*' '*Oui, Cyril. Elle est extrême.*'

It's mid-August. The French landscape is a seared patchwork of brittle yellow and ochre unfolding thousands of feet below, its arteries meandering lines of white rock and expanses of sand. It has a look of something fragile, incendiary, on the edge of disaster. Pensioners are dying, the rivers are dry. That night, with the veranda windows open, we lie in bed listening to the cicadas and the thunderous rumble of a dry electrical storm that flashed through purple and yellow. It circled, receded and returned, but never came closer than the edge of the mountain range that surrounded us.

It took a while to find the road down to the picnic site by the river. Leaving L'Isle sur la Sorgue, three or four avenues lined with poplars led off the main road at a slight angle – the landmarks we'd been told to look for – and we tried all the wrong ones first. We drove into a timber yard, a private garden, and a long way down the most promising track until it ended sharply by a sign marked '*Privée*' and a shuttered courtyard farmhouse. Finally we found the municipal picnic ground and the path that runs beside the river. Cars were parked in the shade of a big willow. A group of people unpacked their lunch by a picnic table. A teenage couple sat on a rock beside the river.

The path is a thin, dusty furrow through dry grass. The river is below us. I can see deep into the water, the marbled gravel bed, and tucked under the shade of the bank two dark grayling moving like flickering candles. Upstream, tall oaks and beeches tower up and out over the river like the buttresses of a cathedral. The sun trickles through a stained-glass window of leaves. Cicadas ratchet the air, a frenzied orgy of noise that builds and subsides in waves. Out of the shade the air is blistering, but the river is sharply cold. Hard orange gravel crunches underfoot. The bed dips and rises in troughs and ridges and is chequered with billowing clouds of green weed, the gravel shining in amber patches between.

I call back to Vicky. 'Fish everywhere!' She looks up from her book, smiles and puts a thumb in the air. I was looking for fish in a French river the day I asked her to marry me. I've been looking for them on and off ever since. The idea is as simple as the reality has proved evasive. We like the sunshine, the landscape, the wine and the food. Now our kids like those things too. But the fishing in France is rubbish, and I need my downtime by the river. Yet here now in every pool or gap in the weed I can see grayling – inert grey shadows stiff against the gravel, or shimmering in the current. This is what I've been searching for.

I wade in further. Shouts and screams come from upstream out of sight, but getting closer. An orange canoe appears. Two teenage boys paddling hard. A moment later another. More follow until the river is a tide of luminous plastic, spiralling or forging downstream. Kids screaming, splashing, laughing. '*Regardez! Un pêcheur! Avez-vous attrapé un poisson, monsieur?*' A guide brings up the rear and cautions the stragglers to take care of the fisherman, not to go too close. He smiles. I smile back, without warmth, sensing the perfect moment dissolve, along with the grayling they will have scared away.

I watch the riverbed come back into focus, peering down to count the empty spaces where the fish were, and when the water finally settles the grayling are still there. I choose a fly, a small goldhead nymph and cast at a good fish. I'm ready for a quick strike but the fish stiffens as the fly passes it. I try again. At the third attempt it slides under the weeds. Ten minutes later more canoes appear – another gabbling flotilla of high-octane kids bent on jeering exchanges with *le pêcheur*. And the grayling are impossible. Not just mildly inscrutable and perverse as they can be sometimes, but plain impossible.

I wade from one pod of fish to the next for an hour or so. Nothing seems to interest them. The canoe flotillas come at intervals of ten minutes, like an invasion. There's just enough time to settle and begin to find the rhythm and suddenly I'm surrounded again, having to pull in the line, get out of the way. Finally, a woman in a bikini appears and starts walking around in front of me – right through the pods of fish – trailing her hands in the water and looking all wistful like she's lost a Cadbury's Flake or something. I reel in, and walk back to find Vicky fast asleep, two pages in. She wakes and squints up at me. 'Catch anything?'

Cyril's card was in the window of the tackle shop in L'Isle. He agreed to meet me by the same picnic ground at ten in the morning, two days' time. Standing at the back of his Peugeot estate he is stocky, has a baby face and smooth, hairless, brown skin. He's wearing tight little khaki shorts, plimsolls, a baseball cap, and a camouflaged fishing waistcoat. I notice his smooth legs and ask if he is into cycling. He says that he isn't but that he shaves them because it keeps him cooler, because he finds hair uncomfortable. I look at my pasty white gorilla legs. I shrug. Cyril's English is poor, so we have a faltering conversation in French. I tell him that I have tried for the fish here already; that I have seen them all over the place, but that they are impossible. '*Non,*' he says, correcting me. '*Très difficile, mais pas impossible.*' He will show me how.

He takes a look at the tapered leader I have on, my own tying. '*Non, non, non.* Fluoro. *Vous avez* fluoro?' I shake my head. '*C'est très, très important.*

Oui, l'ombre est impossible si vous n'avez pas de fluoro. *Bien sûr . . .*' He looks at the end of my line, mutters to himself about the crude diameter of it, and pulls three long lengths of spider's web from the spool hanging off his camo waistcoat. He ties that to the end of my line. He asks to see the flies I have, takes one look and reaches for his own. '*Pas bon?*' '*Non. Trop grand. Trop, trop grand.*' Then he adds with sharp derision, '*Absurde.*' He looks at me and smiles, like I'm going to appreciate his sense of Gallic superiority.

He shakes a minuscule nymph into his hand and ties it on, taking care to let the line hang loose while he spits on it and snugs the knot down. He walks over to the river. A large grayling hovers mid-current in a hole in the weeds. '*Regardez!*' He explains that he will show me why I need such a long tippet. He lifts the rod and hammers it down. The fly enters the water like a tracer bullet, fizzing a line of tiny bubbles out behind it. Quickly Cyril flicks more line loose on to the surface by the descending nymph before raising the rod, and tickling the nymph up and down in the water as it passes the grayling. '*Animation.*'

The grayling lifts for a moment and turns back. Cyril tries again, the same thing happens. He tries a third time and the grayling ignores him. Cyril shrugs. '*Comme ça,*' he says, adding, as he grabs my arm, that I must move from one grayling to the next, right up beside them because they are not timid, and send the fly down on a direct line to the fish, always with animation, always animation.

That final evening Vicky and I walked for a while through the backstreets of L'Isle sur la Sorgue, looking for a café by the water. We found one overlooking the point at which the main river divides around the island that the town is built on – a place called Partage des Eaux. Some kids were swinging on a rope over the river, others splashed in and out of the water from gravel islands in the stream. The boules parc was busy and a jazz band played on the pavement. We sat looking upstream, and as the day ebbed, watched grayling rising under the café lights, dozens of circles fanning outwards and overlapping as the river turned black.

We went back of course. We had to.

M. Arnaud didn't recognise me at first but then I mentioned that I'd been there two years earlier, fishing with Cyril. He looked enlightened and said he'd been trying to place me, that he never forgot a face. I asked after Cyril. M. Arnaud was sorry to say that Cyril had moved away to Lozère. He had finished with guiding altogether. '*Tant pis*. Never mind,' I said. This time I would try to catch them on my own. M. Arnaud smiled. We bought my *permis de pêche* and drove to Partage des Eaux to sit once again on the terrace of Le Pescador.

Patrick and Iona muddy their faces with chocolate

ice cream. We drink coffee. It is midday and Partage is deserted, but as we wait there a few lunchers stroll up the lane to Le Pescador or to sit on the stone benches and look at the river. A wedding party is slowly gathering around the long table, all painted eyebrows, fat bottoms, brown feet squeezed into sandals, neatly pressed shirts, trimmed beards, tidy spectacles. A dozen guests buzz around restlessly, sitting, standing, chatting, embracing, sitting again, standing again. Other guests filter in and each one stirs the table, like a waved hand stirs flies. Finally they seem to settle on a seating plan they are happy with – several of them have moved four times. I notice two anglers fetch a vast cold box from their car to have a picnic with their girlfriends. 'Why don't the kiddies paddle, while I flick a line?' I suggest, giving in to the craving. 'Just for a moment before lunch.'

We find a shingle island in the middle of the stream – a good place for building dams, imprisoning minnows and pretending to read. I wade slowly up the stream to find a grayling. There is a quiet spot in the shade of an oak tree, but it doesn't remain quiet for long. Two fat kids plunge in and out of the river. One throws rocks. He doesn't seem to care where they go and twice he nearly brains his brother. One comes close to hitting me and some of his rocks end up in the pool where I've seen a shoal of the grayling I've come back to conquer. As if I needed it made any more difficult.

The kid seems keen to cause a problem with

someone. His parents are sprawled in camping chairs on an island, both looking the other way. Mum turns at one point to idly check where her kids are, and goes back to her reading when she sees them. Other children start swinging on the rope under the big plane tree in front of Le Pescador. The bravest stands on the handrail, swings far out over the river and drops like a rock. His friend lets his legs drag in the water and waits for the rope to stop, then lets go with theatrical danger. Older teenagers lean on the rail, watching. I reel in. I've revisited the impossibility.

We decide to wade across to the main island to eat our picnic lunch in the shade of the big trees. We find a wall to sit on, dangling our feet over the water.

'Too busy?' Vicky asks. Le Pescador is now a humming throb. The boules parc is filling. Mopeds fart aggressively up and down the lane. A black dog runs back and forth on the weir. An enormous lady in an orange swimsuit is trying to get past it.

'No. I think I like the chaos.' The fat kids are dropping like overripe pears from the tree over the pool where I was fishing, bombing the water. After three bombs the chucker stops and tries to knock his brother out of the tree with rocks.

I went back to L'Isle in the evening – on my own – to find out what happens to the river as it gets dark. I'm hoping that the fish will get a little stupid as the lights go out. Partage is busier than ever, masses of people in the park and restaurants, so I drive past it and down the one-way system along the southern arm of the stream. I park under some trees. The road is empty so I change at the back of the car and two old ladies appear out of nowhere while I have no trousers on. They walk past on their way to Partage chatting animatedly and don't bat an eye. I hear a cough and notice that just downstream from me a fisherman has taken up residence. He has a float, a bunch of worms on the hook and what looks like a heavy uptide bass rod. At least he has less of an idea of what he is doing than I do.

A small boy is bothering him from the terrace of the garden on the other side of the river. The boy is barely old enough to reach his head over the first rail of the fence. 'Monsieur, monsieur,' he says. 'Avez-vous attrapé un poisson?' The man is friendly at first. He says he hasn't had any luck and asks the boy if he knows how to catch them. But the small boy is like a stuck record and he won't go away. 'Monsieur, monsieur.' He asks the same thing again and again. 'Avez-vous . . . ?'

After a while the child's father comes out of the house and drags him away from the fence. But the boy finds his way back again very quickly and the father can only be bothered to call after him abstractedly. The kid has a handful of gravel, which he throws into the river on top of the fisherman's float. 'I am throwing stones,' he says cheerfully. Then, a moment later, 'I am throwing a stick.' The angler asks him not to. His dad calls out that he must not bother the gentleman. The kid runs off and comes back with more gravel. Eventually the fisherman leaves. Meanwhile, I have crouched on the bank under some trees and am trying to tickle a nymph enticingly in front of a grayling. The grayling is not interested. The small boy is, though. He sees me, his next target – '*Monsieur, monsieur.*' I head quickly upriver.

In the shade of the evening the water is cold. I end up shivering in a deep part of the river, my back to a high concrete wall. A shoal of grayling ghosts to and fro across the bed in front of me, grey smudgy shadows in the poor light. While I watch them I hear growling behind me and turn round slowly. It is a fat wolf with dark hair – one I have seen before. The terrace, the garden, the house – suddenly I know where I am. I hear a cough. The owner of the wolf is in a chair on the balcony. She doesn't ask the dog to leave me alone. I slip upstream quietly, up to my armpits to get through the pool. The hound follows me, breathing and sniffing over the wall behind.

All along the stream through the suburbs of L'Isle dogs stick their snouts through gaps in fences and bark or growl as I pass. One sets off another.

The oily, sliding current runs quietly on past sunken wooden punts, under tree stumps and dusty, emaciated bushes. A shoal of a dozen grayling lies under a fig tree that has taken root in a crack in the concrete sheathing. I try for them for over thirty minutes. Twice a fish nods at the fly. Eventually it is too dark to see anything.

We came back to Partage several times during our stay – the same routine of coffee and ice cream, a paddle and a picnic. We bought butterfly nets to catch insects and minnows. We even hired canoes for a morning and floated from the source down to L'Isle, bothering the fly fishermen. I caught a few small fish – one-offs – without establishing a pattern or cracking the code; Iona's catch of minnows beat mine of grayling.

Two days before we were due to leave I went back to M. Arnaud's tackle shop hoping to find some local flies that might unlock the grayling. M. Arnaud came out from the office behind his counter to find me sniffing around his tray of nymphs and asked me how I had got on. I told him I'd caught a few but that it was difficult. He answered quickly, saying something about a good time – about four grayling. But he was difficult to follow. I heard the word 'demang'. Perhaps *demain*? But how can he speak with such certainty about tomorrow? He babbles on. I assume in the end that he must mean he caught four grayling yesterday – an exceptional day. I ask him about where to fish and need to go back to the car to get a map. Vicky comes with me to help me translate. M. Arnaud can't follow the map at all and scribbles instead on Post-it notes, describing *le bassin*, *entre deux ponts*, *interdite ici*, *pas ici*, Super U, *ici bien*. His Post-it scrawls are as unintelligible as he is. Then he moves back to the business of '*demang*' and '*quatre ombres*', points at his watch and counts '*un, deux, trois, quatre*', shows me four fingers and says again '*demang. Après-midi demang, quatre ombres.*'

We chat further and I suggest that the fish near Partage are '*très difficile*' because of all the attention they get. He looks at me amazed. '*Ils sont très difficile partout, monsieur.* Everywhere they are difficult.' He goes to the window behind his counter and notes down some numbers – I assume they are related to large grayling somehow, but he looks up, sees me waiting and explains: they are numbers of fancied horses in this afternoon's race. Our conversation is over. '*À votre service, monsieur. Demang après-midi – quatre ombres.*'

'What was he on about?' I say when we get outside. Vicky explains: some of the best Sorgue anglers, it seems, have special watches that show lunar cycles and atmospheric pressure. Based on the weather and the moon, the watches indicate whether it will be a one-, two-, three- or four-grayling day – a four-grayling day being the best one can hope for. 'He said, "*Les ombres n'aiment pas le mistral.*" The mistral always follows rain. It rained a few days ago, but now the wind has dropped, the pressure is right, the moon is right. Tomorrow good anglers will catch four grayling.' I can't believe it. Watches calibrating moonphase! It isn't just me then. These grayling are officially the most difficult fish on the bloody planet.

We returned on the *demang*, Vicky and the children to go shopping, me to catch *quatre ombres*, like the man said. I was also hoping that the fish in the centre of the town would be more naive than those at Partage on the outskirts – perhaps fewer people will have fished for them.

Vicky and the kids wave goodbye from the footbridge into town. Along one side of the car park is a strip of grass, a row of fig trees, benches and a path along the river. Opposite is the grand stone doorway of the primary school. In the middle of the stream an orange-and-silver grayling shimmies in the sunlight, snaking back and forth, feeding keenly. I sit on a bench to set up my rod. A man walks down the street opposite carrying a box of cakes. The sun has baked fallen figs and dog turds into the dry grass and the air has a rich, tangy smell, so thick I can almost taste it. I kneel between the turds and throw a cast at the grayling. It leaps after the fly taking it in one swift slide and jumps from the bed of the stream. I pull back with overeager surprise, a metallic flash splits the stream, and the grayling comes off.

Downstream, a town drunk comes over to talk. I'm focused on another fish. He tells me there is a large trout in the side stream on the other side of the park, but I say I am after *les ombres*. He drinks his booze from a Powerade bottle in a plastic bag. His little boy is with him – very tidy in a white T-shirt and sandals. The kid chats in a lively sing-song but I don't understand him. When I explain that I'm English he clams up and looks at me suspiciously. His dad tells him to stay where he is and goes off to fetch some figs out of a tree. The boy looks at me, worried. I smile and turn to concentrate on the grayling. Figs start to rain out of the canopy of leaves. The little boy walks over to stand under the tree, but his father tells him to get out of the way. At last the little boy asks his dad why I can't understand him, and his dad explains it is because I am a stranger.

I move away downstream. The path narrows and smells heavily of dog eggs. Lizards rustle through the leaves. I walk by an open window where an elderly lady is cutting bread and watching TV. The river is cooler here in the shade of the tightly packed fig trees. Below the first tree, in a hollow shaded bowl on the bed of the stream, is a nice grayling. I plop a fly on to its nose from behind the tree and the fish takes like it has been waiting all week for such a gift.

Further on, the river opens out into the heat of a busy road. Beside it is a boules courtyard and in the channel are several mill wheels in a row. I walk right to the end of this stream where it meets the main river in a big pool under the road. The pool is full of bottles and bags and under the bridge I find a shoal of big grayling. But I can't fish here. If I hook one I'll never land it, and there is no way in. A sign on the bridge says bathers swim at their own peril and at the risk of death. I walk back upstream and effortlessly catch a grayling from beside the stone wall that lines the river. One more follows back in the shuttered and rich air of the stream by the narrow path.

Finally I see Vicky and the children back in the car park. I whistle to catch their attention.

'*J'ai attrapé trois* of these pesky *ombres*,' I shout.

Iona comes running down the riverbank desperate to show me a grayling above the bridge she's just crossed. From the bridge she points at the fish lying against the pale sand below one of La Sorgue's waterlogged punts. The grayling took first cast. Iona started calling to show Mummy. She ran off the bridge and back again, not knowing whether to get Mummy or just savour the moment. I held the small grayling until she'd done both. We waded further, but there were no more fish.

And then an officious man appeared in white trousers. '*Monsieur, non! Non, ne pêchez pas là!*' He leant over and with great civic authority wagged his finger at me. Patrick and Iona started to giggle and the man walked away up Rue Molière. I looked around for a clue to his problem and found a small sign marked '*Pêche Interdite*'. Oh dear. Illegal fish. It didn't matter – I had my *quatre ombres* and the children had a new joke. They copied him for the rest of the day, wagging their fingers at pretend errant anglers wherever we went.

My Kingdom Come

I HAVE A LONG EVENING AHEAD OF ME AT THE
Sky City Radisson nursing an evil migraine. I cook in
a long, hot shower, drink a Coke, take two Nurofen
and fall asleep under a pillow. I wake two hours later.
Much better. There's little to do. I stroll for a while
around the 'City', watching the other travellers
chasing trolleys noiselessly through the building that
sounds, now I think about it, like an ear infection. All
the shops are closed. At the hotel bar I order a Caesar
salad and chips. Other anglers are easy to spot even
without their rod tubes: marcelled waves of thick
white hair or balding with curls over the ears; checked
shirts, the odd paunch – Scottish salmon refugees on
their way to the Tsar's salmon camp. They're
drinking white wine. I could go over and talk to them,
but for some reason I don't. I hate small talk. And I
don't suppose they'll like the fact that I'm a writer – a
hack. Salmon anglers at expensive camps seem to
resent it the most. I sit on my own reading *Brighton
Rock*.

Back on my bed I listen to the air conditioning. My window looks out into the internal space of the Sky City. The Swedish night is one layer removed – beyond the glass dome. There, in another time zone, the sun has just set, though the sky is still a watery blue. A dotted line of red lights marks the runway. My neutral room has neutral beige walls, an anaesthetised space for identities in transit. The chair is never sat in, but it's mine for the night. Tomorrow it will be someone else's. I watch a couple on a bench inside the dome, surrounded by rucksacks. They curl up and fall asleep, locked together in the same sort of ephemeral privacy.

Early next morning the Skyways check-in is already busy. I find my place in the long queue. Ahead of me are Swedes, Norwegians and Finns, all with short, spiky hair, rugged cheeks, beards. They smoke, wear fleeces, socks inside sandals, carry big PVC holdalls and padlocked plastic rod tubes. They're all in their twenties or thirties. For a moment I wonder if I'm in the wrong queue. These guys look too self-contained for a salmon camp. But then the English and Americans drift in. They're older. In deck shoes and chinos, trailing canvas or leather bags and cases. One overweight and limping. Another wiry and tall with sun-dried skin. He's American. Definitely East Coast. A few wives are along as well. They all greet one another with loud, confident, exclusive laughter. They're old friends. The queue moves slowly.

* * *

In Murmansk the sun ripples heat off the concrete runway. I stand in line, shifting my bags forward with my feet, sweating in the stifling air. Electro-pop plays through tinny, crackling speakers – too soft to hear properly, loud enough to be irritating. Sparrows fly around inside the building stealing onion rings and crisps. Finally, at the front of the queue, the immigration officer examines my passport grimly, holding it upside down under a light. He looks at me and back at the passport, again and again, a farcical ritual that goes on for ever before he stamps it and hands it back without looking.

In the main terminal the enormous departures board – a fading hieroglyph of Soviet aesthetics, functional, muscular, angular – is blank and no longer functions. Outside a Russian in camo is filming an American stretch limousine. The iconography of two cultures. Construction workers mould concrete footings with their hands. By the door a lady unrolls brown paper, cutting it up into smaller rolls which she stacks on end. The amorphous group of fishermen congregates loosely in one corner. Viktor is trying to organise everyone. Smaller groups break off and move to and from the bar, or wander outside. I wonder if Hakan the photographer is here. He might be hanging around like me wondering what the hell he is doing. I walk off to find the loo and Viktor runs downstairs to put a coin in the machine for me. But there are streaks everywhere. No paper, just a bucket of water, which looks ominously like it is designed for bum washing and is second-hand. I change my mind.

I get back and suddenly it's time to go. There is a confusion at the gate to the helicopters. Viktor says I'm supposed to go to the camp at Kharlovka. I'm holding people up. They move past. But the Tsar lives at a different camp, on the Rynda, I say. I thought I must be going there. I left my bags in the Rynda pile and now they are in the Rynda helicopter. At least I think they are. How am I going to interview the Tsar if I'm in a different camp? Viktor looks nonplussed. Then he says it will be fine. I must go with my bags. It will be OK, he thinks. I climb on board the waiting chopper. Everyone else has found a seat. One of the salmon refugees smiles and moves along to make room for me.

It had been hard to get any consensus of opinion about the Tsar. A newspaper had asked me to fly out here and interview this offbeat English millionaire who's saving Atlantic salmon by leasing land off the Russian military. Naturally I asked around a bit first. I found out he made his money binding newspapers with plastic strapping – but that was as far as the facts went. Gossip said he sold his business for a pile of cash and drank too much afterwards, that later he recovered and fell into this Russian salmon project. The rest was James Bond stuff: rumours of struggles with the Russian legal system and a quasi-mafia; a disgruntled competitor taking a contract out on his life, chases through downtown Murmansk. I heard also that the Russians named him the Tsar; that he got on so well up there because he was so much like them.

'Ever been in one of these before?' asks the man next to me. I shake my head. The interior smells of petrol. 'It's an M18. Don't worry. They're bulletproof.' The jet engines whine to a turbine roar and with a lumbering lethargy the thing lifts off the ground, as though winched slowly from above. After ten minutes there was nothing of humanity but for the odd line of telegraph wires running from nowhere to nowhere and long since out of use. Below me, expanses and ribbons of water stretch away to the horizon in all directions, fractals within fractals; a puddle echoing a pool in a river echoing a lake, as far as I can see. The chopper thunders low over this deserted bog. The friendly refugee nods off. After a while I do too.

I wake as we bank in a tight curve. Below us is a cottage set in the crook of a steep bluff beside a waterfall. White water splits over a steeple of dark rocks below it. Beyond, the valley opens up to a rolling slope of moss and scrub through which the Rynda River turns in one long easy meander, vanishing into a steeper-sided canyon. Downstream the waterfall settles into a short, dark pool. The surface is broken with the swelling press of water. And then on it slides, under an amphitheatre of rock. As the chopper turns I catch a glimpse of the river running all the way to the estuary, broadening, until it breaks into a dozen channels over crescent-shaped banks of sand and gravel. A tall figure waves from the edge of the helicopter pad. 'That's him over there,' says the refugee.

In 1998 Peter Power took a forty-nine-year lease on two million acres of the Kola Peninsula, an unspoilt wilderness that after the end of the Cold War had briefly shown the rest of the world its potential as a salmon paradise, before slumping to the edge of disaster. In a brief phone call before my journey Power told me that he simply saved the rivers from the Russians themselves, who had begun to exploit them to extinction: over 75 per cent of the salmon running his four rivers were poached. He dealt with the poachers, recruiting the most notorious of them as head bailiff, and has since declared the place a salmon reserve, pledging to retain its pristine condition, a dream he funds by selling access to visiting anglers.

Power climbs the steps to the landing pad. He greets everyone off the chopper one by one, pausing to chat – like old friends meeting. I hang back. Finally I'm alone and he spots me. Hello. You are? I tell him. You're in the wrong place, he says right away. I assumed I should come here, to interview you. Yes, but I normally park journos down on the Kharlovka for a few days – see them later in the week. Never mind. We'll sort you out. You're here now.

I'm puzzled as to how I can do an interview if I'm in a different valley. Later he says that it is a good thing I'm here. That we'll get to know each other a little before I go to the Kharlovka. It's nearly midnight, but it's never dark up here in July. He nods over towards his log cabin, drawing deeply on a Rothmans. 'You know why I build houses on rivers? I build them because it says I have made my home here. This is my home for the summer and that's very important. It's all about creating happiness. It's all I'm interested in nowadays – creating happiness.' It seems an odd remark. I wonder if I should take notes, and reach for my pad. I stop though, thinking it will make him uneasy, hoping he'll say more. He lights another cigarette. A couple of his guests have joined us. He laughs and says it is his only vice.

The next day Power sees me at breakfast and tells me to get my things together, that he is going to leave me on the Kharlovka for a few days. He'll see me at the end of the week. 'To tell the truth,' he confides, 'I hate all this press business. It makes me nervous. If you're ready in twenty minutes we can get going.'

The Kharlovka camp is a forty-minute chopper ride to the east, but once I get there I find that Hakan has gone one valley further on, to the Litza camp. I have time for a glass of water before the rotors start turning again. Finally I'm dropped on a stone beach on the inside bend of a turn in the Litza River. I've come to Russia to interview a man who has left me at the furthest edge of his fiefdom and my notebook contains one enigmatic remark, scribbled on the airlift over here, about creating happiness. A dog comes towards the chopper barking and wagging its tail. Forget the interview. There is nothing to do now but fish. And why not? I am standing by one of the best salmon rivers in the world, unlikely ever to get here again.

A handful of tents is set among scrub along the edge of the stone beach – the guide's quarters, a kitchen, two sleeping tents and at a decent distance another tent built over a hole in the ground. It's here I catch up with Hakan, the photographer for my interview. He'd been wondering where I'd got to. He'd been up the hill taking pictures for most of the day. He was at the camp with Harry, who was fast asleep, and Harry's father James, who was sending out a few casts over the pool by the camp, trying to cover a line of rocks at the tail where he'd seen a salmon jump. We drank a few beers and later we fished through the sunlit night.

The sun dropped to just below the western ridge, leaving the valley in a permanent dusk, and the eclipse light softened everything – the air, the sound of the river and the outlines of rocks and trees. Under a tall cliff the water turned a milky blue and seemed to move in slow motion. A fish showed itself where a chute of lively current came off the riffle above and settled into a rolling boil. I waded over and covered the spot several times, but I think the fish had been running. It was four in the morning. When I turned upstream I saw a splash a long way up the half-mile riffle that separated the cliff from the camp. The fish would rest when it reached the top, I thought, so I walked back upriver to get above it. Just before dawn I caught a six-pounder from the tail of the camp pool. The fish turned up through the water, the line tightened and my salmon was on. As the sun climbed to become a sliver of orange shimmering over the blue hill, the river seemed to wake. The sound of running water grew crisper as the edges, colours and lines sharpened with the brightening day. It gave me the distinct feeling that I had been fishing in my sleep, that I was waking to find a salmon on the line.

After a few hours' sleep I ate lunch with the bailiff – fish soup and a plate of spaghetti, three dog's-dick sausages dropped on top, with Russian tomato chutney for flavour – before heading downstream to meet the others. I followed the bailiff. He did this walk every day, like the bailiffs on Power's other rivers, to keep poachers away. He liked to walk the ridges above the valley, so we parted company once I knew which way to go. As I came over a rise of land I saw Harry on the far bank. He was half a mile away but I was sure he was into a fish. By the time I reached him it had been played, released and he was into another. 'It was about sixteen pounds,' said James, who was fishing a run on the near bank with focused determination. 'That one looks smaller.' I got the impression Harry was catching too many.

That night we were airlifted back to the Kharlovka camp, and after supper Harry and I went out to the Falls Pool. I had lost touch with time, grabbing sleep when I could – in the chopper, in the bar – but Harry's enthusiasm was infectious and someone had to keep him company. The falls are a barrier to migrating salmon until the river warms enough for the fish to make the jump – before that the salmon stack in there like a bank holiday traffic jam. I fished off the steep rocks on the far bank, pulling popper flies over the jumping salmon. Harry caught two, while I turned and missed the same number. Dice don't roll evenly with salmon and the moment can soon evaporate. A brief rush of activity – a swirl by the fly, or a pull on the line – may go as quickly as it comes. And after there is nothing, except a sense that it is all over. I don't suppose I've ever fished for salmon without feeling that I'd missed my chance or that it would never come. But here on the Kharlovka at midnight, as the falls thunder behind me and salmon turn, flop and crash the full length of the pool, expectation is making my hair stand on end. Harry's reel shrieks in the half-light and, dancing across the rocks in pursuit of another salmon, he shouts over to me: 'You can sleep when you're dead!' James was told about Harry's two midnight fish at breakfast, that one of them weighed twenty-five pounds. He laughed and shrugged. 'Some of us just get to pay,' he said.

* * *

Days at Kharlovka bleed seamlessly one into the next.
Hakan and I fished and slept, and then one afternoon
(I think it was afternoon) Power reappeared. A buzz
of excitement and animated rushing around accom-
panied him wherever he went, as though some
general had made a surprise visit to the front. He
dropped past our hut, suggested we had time for a
quick drink, but that we should be ready to go in
twenty minutes. I threw my bags together in a hurry
and walked to the main hut, only to find him tucking
into the fresh crab starter laid out on one of the picnic
tables. Eat plenty, he said, as it would be all I'd get
that night. Then he turned to the pilot. 'Let's stop at
Russian on the way home.'

'You know, I love this,' Peter said later, lighting his
cigarette and gesturing that I should go ahead and fish
while he sat. Misha, the manager of the camp on the
Zolotoya River, brought him a chair and a coffee. 'I
have to admit I love the whole travelling entourage
thing. I feel like some kind of feudal lord dropping in
by surprise around the estate.' Peter smoked his
cigarette and drank his coffee. Hakan sat with him.
Peter examined Hakan's dog tag and said that by
rights the lower half should be sent to the mother. 'It
should go always to the mother. There's nothing like
a mother. God bless her, I hope mine is listening.' He
finished his coffee and cigarette, and watched me fish
for a few moments longer.

The Zolotoya is a small river, a goat's leap wide
and only a few miles from source to sea. Russian Pool

is deep but short, a resting place for salmon before their ascent up an immense staircase of boulders and tumbling water that goes on for over a mile until the river flattens out again high above. 'Last cast!' Peter shouted. I pulled a yard or two more line from the reel. I'd seen a tail flick above the surface of the glassy water where the pool ran out to the next rapid downstream, and wanted to swing a fly across that spot before reeling in. I laid the line out down to the rocks at the tail, a fish turned, my line straightened and I was in. The salmon crashed across the surface, leapt once, turning full circle around the fixed point of taut line, and hit the water with a heavy crack, before pulling up and down in the confined space like a dog on a long leash. The fish was fresh, silver and full of beans and wouldn't give in. Finally, though, I beached it on the rocks, turned out the fly and Hakan snapped a picture. The fish scythed its tail strongly and faded into the dark pool. At that moment the Zolotoya River seemed to me the most perfect place I'd ever fished for salmon. 'Fantastic,' said Peter. 'Fantastic. I'll give that fourteen pounds.'

We flew from the Zolotoya back to Peter's home on the Rynda River, straight into the midnight sun, banking hard left and low out of the valley, and snaking along a ribbon of water that shone against the low light. As we passed over and the lakes flashed from silver to dark green I could see they were pocked with the rings of rising trout.

* * *

The week had blurred with constant daylight, and I had no idea what day it was when Peter took me with him to find his Swedish and Norwegian campers. I was vaguely aware though that time was running out: my notebook contained a few scrawls and no more. Peter wanted to cheer his intrepid guests up with an airlift relief flight of beer and sausages. I hoped this was the moment when I'd get something approaching an interview. 'We will start by finding Vidar,' said Peter. 'A fantastic man. You won't find the Brits doing what he's doing. Living the life of the river – out there in the wilderness, just fishing. We'll get a gift hamper together. What will Vidar like? Steaks? Beer?'

Vidar and his friends were pleased to see us. Peter brought out a crate of beer, bacon, sausages and Mars bars and indicated that there was more up by the chopper. 'Coca-Cola?' asked one of them running uphill. He wasn't even slightly disappointed to find there was only beer and that it was warm.

The upper reaches of the salmon rivers braid on the inland moors to become an endless and intricate maze of water – rapid streams linking slow pools and lakes, and meanders turning in on themselves like the Celtic patterns in an illuminated manuscript. The brown trout here have been undisturbed since the ice age, and without stocking and overfishing have grown enormous – worth the pain and privation.

We stopped in other spots to fish, but halfway

through the day Peter began to cough. He started to sweat and after a little food said he wasn't feeling too well. He lay down on the grass by the river and fell asleep. After a few moments the pilot – he was called Sacha – came over fussing that Peter had fallen asleep on the grass and would get cold. He spoke quietly with Vassili, another guide who had flown with us. Vassili felt Peter's forehead. They spoke some more. They looked unsure of whether to disturb him, but genuinely concerned about his health. After a while Sacha returned to the chopper to arrange some cushions, and Vassili shook Peter awake and took him back to sleep there. There was nothing to do now. They wanted him to rest, so I slept too, with my head on a rock by the river.

I woke an hour later to the sound of anxious voices again. The sky was black to the north of us. With a storm approaching we had to race back to camp ahead of it. Peter was pale. He had stopped talking and had a fever. His lungs sounded awful.

Back at the Rynda he was taken down to his cottage. The doctor was called, and Peter simply disappeared. Along with him so did my chances of an interview. I had a few notes about the feudal role and the love of mothers, a brief hint that he was someone who inspired real affection in those who worked for him and a good travel piece about salmon fishing – but no interview with the enigmatic millionaire. Whenever I asked after him I was told he was not well, and shouldn't be disturbed. Would

I get a chance to see him again? Kola, who managed the camp, shrugged and said he'd see what he could do.

Late that night I was making notes in the dining hut and chatting with Hakan. All the salmon refugees were in bed. Kola joined us, bringing with him a bottle of Ukrainian vodka. The vodka was like gunpowder – a mixture of vodka, honey and pepper. 'A real treat,' said Kola. He told us about the old Russia, his life in the army, and how he went AWOL to see Pink Floyd in Moscow. He was caught at the railway station and sent to prison. They made him throw tyres over a wall for ten days. He said things were better now. I asked after the camp, how he and the others enjoyed it. Kola shrugged, as though the answer were obvious. 'The workers like it here,' he said matter-of-factly. 'He looks after us, and pays us well. The other camps in Russia have American guides, but why? Why would you go to Russia and have American guides? What's the point?'

These rivers, Kola told us, had been at the brink of destruction before Power showed up. But the one-off poachers had been sent packing, the criminal gangs prosecuted. The count of young fish had doubled in the last few years, the returns of adult fish had quadrupled. Nowhere else were whole river systems protected like this, nowhere else was the landscape so unspoilt.

I wondered what day it was, how long I had left. One day, Kola said. With Peter laid up I might as well spend it fishing. 'Anyone fishing the Zolotoya tomorrow?' I asked as casually as I could. Kola smiled. He knew what I was after. It was in the rota for two of the refugees, but they didn't want to fish there. They thought it was too small. 'If you drop me at the top, would I make the estuary by evening?'

'If you move fast,' said Kola.

It was simply the best day's salmon fishing I've had or am ever likely to have. Hakan and I fished from the small lake that feeds the Zolotoya all the way to the estuary, hopscotching the likely spots, occasionally at a half-canter to cover the ground. I caught four salmon. Hakan caught two or three. My first had sea lice on it and the lice had not even lost their tails: this fish had run the whole river in less than a day. They were all like this: a silver so bright it hinted at blue, and with heavy, just-off-the-sea shoulders.

At one point the river dropped steeply away and to follow it we had to climb over a steep, domed hill. The grass on top was scrawny and dry and whisked back and forth in the wind. Wild flowers grew in the lee of rocks or dips in the ground and broke the surface into a mottled dubbing of colour. I could see inland to the lake and the low craggy hills beyond, from which the headwaters trickled and coalesced to form the Zolotoya, all the way down to the estuary where the river settled into a broadwater over yellow sandbanks. An entire catchment in one panoramic sweep, as unspoilt as any river I will ever stand beside.

In the evening Sacha took us all down to the Rynda fishing village at the mouth of the river. The Rynda bailiff and his wife lived there watching over the estuary, in one of the old wooden houses. The buildings nearby stood empty and derelict. The bailiff's wife sat us down at a table laid out with pancakes and jams over a patterned cloth hemmed with glass beads. We drank tea and chatted politely, as Vassili translated. On the wall was a picture of the same village, but full of people – a faded, black-and-white image. They wore clothes from another era. Vassili explained that the village and others like it were founded on the instructions of the Tsar in the late nineteenth century to populate the area and prevent the Norwegians from colonising. The villagers lived on fish and what little they could glean from the tough landscape – the same berries that made our jam were a staple in their diet. The revolution came and went unnoticed in this forgotten part of the empire until some psychotic mandarin became aware of the existence of these villages – where the people were technically still loyal to the Tsar. A gunboat was sent along the coast. Our bailiff's grandparents survived because on the day the boat came they were in the hills picking berries. They returned to find everyone dead.

I went to look around the other houses. Though they had been empty for over eighty years I felt as though I was trespassing on private property – not that I was unwelcome, but that I was in someone's house, that they had only stepped out for a minute.

In one building the old ladder staircase was strong enough to climb. On the first floor a piece of string hung from a nail on the wall: knotted at intervals in the string were the desiccated tails of salmon. The same in the opposite corner, though the string had broken and rotted. Whoever had lived here had hung fish across the room to dry or to smoke them. I wondered if these salmon had been netted and hung up on the morning of the massacre. And the salmon surging up the Rynda, as abundantly as they had ever done, seemed such a strong link with the past.

My bags packed, and ready with pad and pencil, I sat on my bed hoping for a call. Kola knocked, and said Peter was well enough to see me. I found him sitting up, eating eggs. His voice came from a long way off, as if through a thick door. 'You know, I've been really ill,' he said. 'I know you want to talk. Come in. Sit down.' He finished his breakfast, and then brought a coffee with him to sit next to me by the window. The doctor had him on a cocktail of pills. He coughed. 'I know I shouldn't smoke.' He lit a cigarette. He looked out the window for a moment, at the white falls of the Rynda below the cottage.

'I've realised now I'm sitting on something very, very special ... It is more important than anything else I've ever done in life. Nothing compares with this.

Voltaire ended *Candide* saying, "Don't forget to tend the garden." I know what he meant. Imagine if in a couple of hundred years' time this can still be the Atlantic Salmon Reserve, the home for salmon. Imagine that.'

The Year of the Big Fish

The Nine Hatches' Trout

WE PARKED AT SWAN'S ISLAND AND WALKED DOWN-
stream, crossing the meadow at the U-bend, heading
straight for Chinese Bridge. There's little point in
following the river round the U-bend – it has been
dredged so hard I've never seen the bottom of the
stream, even in the worst droughts. Of all the parts of
the Frome that have been dredged, this might be the
most appalling. The dredger went crazy, like he hated
the damn river, and just wanted to keep digging for
the sheer destructive hell of it. The water is slow and
dark and there are no fish in it. The edges are puddled
bare by the ducks that flight here, thinking it's a
pond. The water looks like it might hold pike, but it
doesn't. There's nothing for pike to eat.

Chinese Bridge was obviously here when the
dredger came because there is a thin shelf of gravel a
few feet wide right underneath it, rising up from the
dark like an atoll off the seabed. We crossed the

bridge, which wobbles underfoot – the boards look more rotten every year – and turned downstream. All the way to within fifty yards of Nine Hatches the river lies in the same bottomless trench. The brick-and-metal structure of the hatches must have been a problem for the dredger though. He couldn't easily reach the stream here, and couldn't dig the bed out from under them. So he left the river alone and moved on, sparing fifty yards of the Frome as God made it – fast and shallow. There is a fish that owns those fifty yards. I knew it was there. I'd seen it the year before and the year before that.

Approaching from upstream is a problem. Just above the hatches a concrete sill forms the northern edge of the channel and the only easy route down the bank. The sill leads to a flood relief cut – when levels build up in the main river water spills over the sill into the cut and off into a carrier stream that runs parallel. The concrete sill therefore forms the upper edge of a staircase of three concrete ponds, designed, I presume, to allow salmon free passage from the carrier stream to the spawning grounds that were once there but have now been ripped out by the dredger. Anyway, walk along the sill and a fish in this short oasis of water will be spooked.

I explained to Paul that we'd have to shimmy down the steep slope into the flood relief cut and back up the other side. It was about two thirty or three in the afternoon. We'd been fishing all day, but I had timed this part of the day well. The mayfly hatch was thickening. There were even a few on the relief channel which was hardly flowing. When I looked up from the bottom of the cut to the sill on the edge of the river, I saw a cloud of mayflies in the lee of a hawthorn bush and more lifting off the river into the air.

We climbed the bank, through nettles and brambles and over a barbed-wire fence, walked into the field for a few yards and came round at the hatches from downstream. The whole thing seemed an extreme ritual to Paul. I hadn't told him what we were looking for, though I think by now he had an idea it was something unusual.

I crawled up to the edge and took a look around the iron upright. The fish, which is usually hard to see, tends to lie in a deeper slot under reeds the far side of where the flow rips through to the hatches below. I've never seen it rise, and always struggled to get a nymph to it. The two times I'd seen it before I'd tried and the fish had vaporised after a few casts. But today the trout was lying over the shallows on the near side, its dorsal fin just breaking the surface. 'There it is,' I said.

'Bloody hell!'

'It's the biggest I've ever seen in the Frome. Look at it. It's a submarine. It's half out of the water.'

In previous years I'd only seen it deep and in the shadows, and so the fish had remained something of a phantom. Now, close to the surface in hard sunlight, it seemed stunningly substantial. As we knelt there, somewhat awestruck, the fish took a lunge to its left and sucked a mayfly off the surface, turned back and did the same to the right. It resumed its lie, then moved hard across the stream again. A mayfly was two yards away, in the middle of the river. The trout took it, then carried on up the centre of the stream tipping up for two more flies, before turning and catching another on the way back down. At the last it slurped at the surface like a wet, sloppy kiss, the only noise to break the silence as my world closed in on the fish. 'It's feeding like a pig,' I whispered. 'Troughing all over the river. Look at it. Left. Right. All over the place.'

'You gonna catch it then?' It wasn't easy to get the fly to a place where the fish would see it. I cast to the right as the fish took a fly to the left; dropped one to the left as it swam upstream. And I was so paranoid about spooking it I paused between each cast to let the universe settle down. At last one caught its attention. The trout turned to the left, drifted downstream a foot or two and confidently rose to the fly. I struck and flossed the beast's teeth.

'Bollocks. Too early! Too early!' The great trout swirled and dived under the weeds like a plane dropping through clouds, leaving a weakening vortex of surprised water to drift downstream. 'Hell. I don't think it'll come back. That's it for another year.'

'Leave it for a minute,' said Paul. 'I need a ciggy. I'll roll and smoke one. Bet you he's rising again when I've finished.' I wanted to believe him, but I'd felt that trout and it had felt me. I didn't think it would feed again for a week.

I leant back against the hatch upright and waited – not for the fish, but for Paul to finish his smoke. The trout reappeared. It took a fly. Paul wouldn't let me cast though. He said he had to finish his cigarette before I put my line on the water. He smoked it slowly.

The fish was feeding confidently by now. It took my next cast – and I missed the strike. God knows how. The trout bolted under the weeds once more while mayflies sailed on past. I turned to Paul and shrugged. I was too sick to say anything. Paul pulled out his baccy pouch and said, 'I fancied another anyway.' And while now it should have seemed doubly impossible that the great trout would feed again, I was happy for Paul's optimism to carry the moment. I laid the rod down in the grass, tied on a new fly – just in case the trout might have wised up to this one – and turned to chat to the smoking seer. I didn't dare look round. As Paul took his last drag and stubbed the butt out on the steel of the hatch bridge he nodded at the river behind me.

'It's been back for a minute now. I'd smoke a third if it wouldn't make me sick. Still think you should leave it for another minute or two.' We timed it. Three minutes – one for luck. By now the trout was up and at the mayflies like nothing had happened and this time I counted two elephants before striking. For a very brief moment it felt exactly like I had lifted the fly into a floating log – the trout simply dropped downstream with the current, as if investigating this weird sensation. But I had leapt up and was standing above the fish as it drifted by me towards the hatch. Suddenly it started to gyrate. It was spinning over and over against the resistance, but remained a dumb, directionless weight on the line. I pulled as hard as I dared to shock the fish out of its crocodile roll.

'If it goes through the hatch I'm dead.'

'If it goes through the hatch,' said Paul, 'I'm going in after it.'

The trout peeled away and forged upstream. 'I'm going up the sill, Paul. You wait here this side of the cut. If I get him into the concrete pond he can't get away even if he breaks the line.' I hopped over the cut. The trout was swimming heavily in circles. I pulled at the fish like it was on a leash. The trout swam with the current right at the cut, and flopped over the sill into the pond.

I'm not sure if I regret landing it there – looking back the fish seemed suddenly so out of place. Paul reckoned it was cheating, but then he'll say anything to wind me up. The trout was the biggest I'd ever caught though – well over five pounds. I held it in the current above the sill until it dropped from my grasp to the stream bed where it lay for a few hours – I kept checking.

A year on it's still there. I mentioned the fish to the only other person I know who bothers with that spot. He'd seen it but had never caught it. A few days ago he wrote to say that he had now – and that it was the largest trout he'd ever caught too.

The Norfolk Sea Trout

I stopped my car under the yew tree by the old gatehouse near Mundford. I like to stop and take a look off the bridge when I cross it. It's private water, but there is a deep pool downstream of the bridge. The fish tend to hover just back from the gravel shelf at the upstream edge where the current ripples off the shallows and drops into the hollow of the pool. Or at the back, where the main current peels either side of an overgrown shoal in the stream.

I was driving back from Dorset with Paul. We stopped for the time it took him to roll and smoke a ciggy. We watched the trout rise to mayflies. I crossed the road to have a look off the upstream side. Here the river is straight and broad, and shows plenty of evidence of the keepering that makes it so expensive to fish. I looked upstream for a while, for rising trout in the distance. Then I looked down, and right underneath me lay an enormous fish. Out of all proportion to the river, it was like something from another geological age. It was a sea trout. I called Paul over, but as he crossed the road the fish dropped back under the bridge and out of sight. We waited for a while, but it didn't come back.

* * *

The Year of the Big Fish

Perhaps thirty years ago Mr Gurney opened a fish shop opposite the garage in Brancaster, down the road from my parents' house. It was a tiny shed of a shop, no more room inside than for Gurney the fishmonger and one or two customers. These were always women. I remember a friend of my mother's coming back from Gurney's one day and confiding too loudly for me to miss that Gurney was 'a bit dishy'. It seemed that most of the middle-aged women of north Norfolk had noticed, and Gurney was doing a hell of a trade as a result. Queues of women would gather on the road outside, waiting their turn for fish and fantasy. I didn't mind being dragged along there because Gurney always had a crate of the most incredible sea trout. White as the moon, sandy and fat. Anything from four to eight pounds. Occasionally bigger. Once I saw a twelve-pound fish in there. I asked him where they came from. From the beach, he said. The sea trout were there all summer, feeding off the Norfolk coast. It seemed a bloody shame to me that such magnificent fish should fall to a beach net, but I was amazed to find they were taken from my doorstep.

After that discovery I used to cycle down to the salt marsh and try to catch one on a spinner. I had a blue-and-white Devon Minnow and I pulled it up and down those creeks but I never touched a fish. I saw one jump once where the harbour creek crosses the sand to the open sea. And years later when I was walking from the harbour along the sea wall –

without a fishing rod – I saw a pair come racing up one of the salt creeks on the high tide. They ghosted along the edge of the creek, all the way to the top, and then back down again on the far side. I ran after them, hoping somehow I'd pick up a clue as to how and when to catch them. But they vanished out of the end of the creek as quickly as they had appeared. That was twenty years ago, and the secret to catching sea trout here took more unlocking than I had time for then or on my occasional visits to Norfolk in the years following.

The theory is that these sea trout are Northumbrian and Scottish east-coast fish from rivers like the Tweed and Till. They feed through the year in a big clockwise circle of the North Sea, the summer leg of which takes them along the north coast of Norfolk before they run back up the east coast to spawn in the rivers they came from. That may be partly true. But I think that many of these sea trout are not visitors at all. They're Norfolk sea trout. They've come from Norfolk's rivers and are feeding along the coast before returning to Norfolk's rivers. I've heard stories of Ouse fishermen catching them by accident, of sea trout turning up every year in the Wissey, or the Nar.

And why wouldn't sea trout be running the Ouse? If I lay a map out it's obvious all of the rivers running into it from the south-east are chalk streams – two dozen of them from the Oughton in Hertfordshire to the Babingley north of King's Lynn. The coast itself

has half a dozen tiny chalk streams running off the
north Norfolk downs straight into the sea. I was
within a few hundred yards of the smallest of these
when I saw that pair of fish on the salt marsh. Off the
east coast the Wensum and Bure have as many sea-
trout rumours attached to them as the Ouse. Pike
anglers catch sea trout in the Broads. Kids catch sea
trout on worms in Norwich.

'How big was it then?' Paul asked. I told him it was
closer to fifteen than ten, but he didn't believe me.

A month later, on the day the coarse-fishing season
opened, I suggested to my son Patrick that we walk
the dog along the Nar near Setchey off the A10. I'd
take a small spinning rod and stop for a cast if we saw
a pike. The Nar here runs in a trapezoid channel high
above the surrounding Fens. It is a great spot for pike.
There are chub in it too, and shoals of roach and
perch.

We got out of the car, and before letting the dog out
I went to have a look over the edge. As I leant on the
parapet a fish swam out from a deep forest of weed
downstream of the bridge. It turned in a slow circle
right underneath me and swam back into the forest. I
saw it for only a few seconds, but enough to catch the
square, black tail and an adipose fin the size of a
cherub's plonker. It was another biblical sea trout.

I put a fly over the spot once a day for the next five
days hoping it would come back. It didn't.

* * *

It started raining – a heavy summer shower. I rang Rosie. She lives by a small, sandy brook that colours up well in a downpour – enough to make casting a fly in daylight worthwhile. It's only a few feet wide and is hemmed in by heavy brambles. It would be impossible to fish it in the dark. Rosie's house is a few hundred yards above the tide and her meadows run down to the sea wall. I've caught trout in there down as far as the sea gate. I was sure that sea trout must run it.

I parked outside Rosie's house and walked down-hill across the meadow to the river. The tide was out and the stream was running fast. I worked my way down to the sea gate, casting where I could. The stream runs in a trough a long way below the bank. In places there are gaps in the brambles where it is possible to find a footing, lean out over the water and get something of a downstream cast in. But for much of the way the river is hidden behind the bramble walls and vaulted with fallen branches. For shy sea trout fresh off the tide it must be bloody heavenly.

At the sea gate I hope for a take. A big fish took my fly there once and ever since I've wanted to try it again. It is possible, with a really good cast, to lay a straight line between the reed beds and drop the fly above the pipe that runs into the salt marsh. Something grabs it. My heart jumps. It pulls back but gives in too quickly. I can tell right away it's a small trout. It jangles around on the end of the line. I put it back and climb the steps to fish the pool on the other side of the sea wall. The view opens out and stretching away to the horizon is the smudgy, mauve and green marsh, smelling of mud and fresh air and salt. The creek is no more than a chrome trickle over shining mud, but below me the sea gate forces the fresh water of the stream into a deep hole. I slither down the greasy bank and cast a long line across the tail of the pool to bring it up and through the faster, darker water. Nothing. I throw a few more casts, but I've covered the spot. The day ends like all my other experimental sea-trout forays on the north coast of Norfolk: with failure, but failure in a beautiful setting.

On my way back upstream I try one more cast, in one of the few places I can throw a good line, towards a muddy streak of water dribbling out of the flighting marsh on the opposite bank. The fly swings round slowly. I don't move it at all. I just let it hang in the current . . .

A blurred shape lifts off the sandy bed. Time slows. The trickle of water turns to white noise. The shape tips under the fly and opens, turning white. The seconds unzip, open down the middle and unfold. Legs heavy, utterly transfixed, I lift the rod as the white hole closes and sinks back into the ochre water. My world implodes, the river erupts, the seconds zip closed again, tighten upandrushforwardandthis glorious, enormous, gigantifecking sea trout goes nuclear.

The Big Laxa Trout

'As you can see,' said the taxi driver, 'our landscape is very naked. Many people land here and feel they have come to the moon.' I rolled the window down and back up to clear the streaks of rain, and watched the bare, rock-strewn land roll by. Reykjavik was across the bay. The road stretched away like a piece of black tape.

Perhaps there are worse ways of starting a fishing trip. It's just that Ronnie couldn't think of any. He asked if I could bring a few more trout rods out when I joined them. I asked how many he'd broken. Fourteen, he said. And maybe a couple of ribs: Tony's ribs. Ronnie only had some glass in his head. The car landed on top of the rods. 'So it's not that the fish are too big, then?' I asked.

Later, from the twin-prop Fokker, I saw a glacier through the thin clouds, an immense tongue of dirty white ice licking down the spoon of the valley, running out into a lake of milky water. The plane started to shake in the turbulence of a northerly rearing over the mountain shelf and we dropped to Akureyri. White ice gave way to stark hills, then to meadows in a random patchwork, isolated farmsteads and poppled rivers sweeping from side to side under cut gravel banks.

When I arrived at Randholer Laxardal, Ronnie was out exploring with a rod he'd taped back together. Tony came limping out of his room, a little pale, clutching his side and grimacing.

The Year of the Big Fish

The lodge was above a lake – a sheet of water three hundreds yards wide, disappearing beyond sight upstream, the Laxa i Adaldal pouring out at its lower end through a tight gorge. Only later when I got in to wade did I realise that the lake was shallow and on the move. The surface was flecked with foam and slid under me like a walkway. Fish were rising everywhere, but only once or twice in each place. Without landmarks it was difficult to pinpoint the rises, so I waded and waited. If I stood still for a few minutes a fish might rise nearby. There were hundreds of tiny midges standing high on the surface tension. The trout rose at one in twenty, and the rise forms were tiny.

The river flattened to a glass calm as the wind dropped. The drag was impossible. At last I hooked one. It leapt straight up through a hole in the water, launched like a rocket. Then it jumped over and over, sending ripples to the bank fifty yards behind me. A few minutes later I caught another that shook in the still air, with a sound like the theatrical wobble of cardboard used to create distant thunder. I've never caught stronger trout. They were silver like sea trout, hard and deep with small heads and a pepper garnish of black spots.

The morning was bright and Tony decided over breakfast that once the aspirin took effect he'd be able to join in. Bjarni took us upstream to a broad run smudged where water peeled around submerged rocks. Within half an hour the air was hot. Swarms of heather flies buzzed in the lee of volcanic outcrops.

Ronnie waded out to cover a very large trout all of us had seen jump.

Tony was below me on the edge of the river watching Ronnie when a fish moved upstream of him. It could have been any size. Tony, hardly moving, covered it with a short cast. The water boiled and a trout made off across the river in one long, remorseless run, right under Ronnie's left shoulder. Bjarni laughed and said that it wasn't a small fish. Tony was rooted to the spot by his injuries and started to curse. 'Come back, will you? For heaven's sake, this is ridiculous. Oh crumbs. It's swimming away again.' The trout wouldn't come in. Every time it reached shallow water it turned and bored away. And each time it grew. At first it was two pounds, then three. When Bjarni finally netted it, it was nearly twice that size – two feet long and five pounds. Tony held it reluctantly for a picture, complaining about his ribs, and said it just happened to be the largest trout he'd ever caught on a dry fly.

Beyond the next bend I saw a fish in rough water a long way out across a shallow fan of volcanic gravel. The fish chased the fly downstream and exploded with fury when I set the hook. The trout leapt sideways – it was huge – skipped its tail across the water, dropped, ran twenty feet, boiled at the surface and was gone. I stood there watching the dying wake and wondered what the hell had happened.

The riffle quietened after that, though trout moved occasionally, boiling at the surface loud enough that

The Year of the Big Fish

I heard rises before I saw them. Suddenly a large fish moved under the rod tip. On the fifth cast he took – another strong fish, silver and deep and tireless. It took ages to get him close, and each time he pulled out line again. 'He's about two pounds,' said Ronnie, who'd crept down the bank behind me.

'If he's two pounds I'll buy you a Ferrari. That fish is nearly four pounds.' When we got him in the net we agreed on three and a half. Orri told us this was average size for the trout here, that several thousand were caught each year and that many, many of the bigger ones were killed – a difficult set of statistics to process. What river can sustain that? But slipping the cold and slimy fact of the matter back into the water, I started busily to revise my concept of how good trout fishing can get.

Back at the lodge I looked into the fishing log: the season began on 29 May. On that day one man caught eleven trout for over fifty pounds – just under five pounds a fish. Between then and the end of July, 1,395 trout had been caught, and the largest weighed seven pounds. Several more were over six. The same happens year in, year out. Bjarni said he'd fished here since he was a lad. It is as good now as it ever was.

We were sitting by the windows of the lodge looking out over the home pool, wondering what monsters were out there. I could see the occasional boil on the far side, as though some paddle had swept under the surface. A tongue of wind licked across the pool, the surface flattened again briefly then stirred to a ripple. By the time we'd finished lunch small whitecaps frothed against the rocks on the south-east shoreline. The afternoon was dead. Not a fish stirred.

Monday morning dawned calm and warm. A few trout were moving in the flat water. By the time I'd put a line out the wind had stiffened, and the fish were down. The snake in this Arctic Eden was wind. When the wind got up the heather flies wouldn't swarm. Without them the fish hardly rose at all.

For two days the wind blew. Tony was happy to nurse his ribs, but Ronnie and I got the shack-nasties and Bjarni took us for a drive. Out in the real world, coachloads of tight polyester slacks and fossilised hairdos swarmed like ants over lava beds, hot mud and volcanic springs. By nightfall I was happy to wrestle the wind come what may. And in every lull we got into monsters. Tony beat his five-pound record by a pound. I hooked a trout that ran a hundred yards like a bonefish before bending the hook; fast, furious, unbelievable sport.

But Wednesday was something else entirely. We fished a run which Bjarni had warned us was good. It was quiet at first and I took some pictures of Ronnie creeping up the bank looking for rises. I saw the first through the viewfinder, and pointed it out. Ronnie hooked the trout: a modest four-pounder. I put the camera down and caught one too. Tony wandered up and did the same. By now a line of large trout were rising in a narrow seam of current. The drag was awkward and each trout needed work. Ronnie caught another of four pounds, Tony one of three and a bit, and I got one more too, before the rise petered out. Six fish for about twenty-three pounds.

Finally Tony mentioned a fish he'd tried for and missed downstream. I went to have a look, and as I walked down the bank I saw it rise exactly where Tony had said it would be. The nose came up and over my fly. The trout, hardly knowing it was hooked, wallowed briefly in the shallow water and swam lazily towards me, passing between where I stood and the bank. It was huge. As soon as it saw me it lit out of the pool and ran for miles. I held the rod high and ran too, stumbling on to the bank, finally catching it a long way downstream. The trout was over two feet long. Its adipose fin was the size of my thumb. I lay it in the shallows and took pictures. It must have been six pounds. It was the largest wild brownie I'd ever caught.

Somewhat dazed I walked back to tell the others. The ground felt softer. I didn't need to fish any more that day. It couldn't get better. I noticed, in passing, another fish rising in exactly the same spot. 'Let Ronnie have it,' I thought. 'It can't be as big.' Ronnie was happy to give it a go. He'd had nothing more upriver. He muttered something about it being a minnow, but had a cast anyway. I got the take on film – Ronnie open-mouthed and paralysed as the trout made for the horizon. 'Ayeeeee! What the hell? Help! Come back. Help!' The fish ran deep into the backing. Ronnie scrambled to the bank. I ran after him and grabbed a net. As I tried to ambush the monster in the shallows, Ronnie said helplessly over and over, 'That's not a trout. It's a salmon. That's not a trout. It's a salmon.'

It was a trout though. The largest trout Ronnie had ever caught. An ounce or two heavier than mine.

Blame it on the Boogie

Angel Delight

'LET'S GET DOWN THERE AND GET AMONGST IT.'
Rich is sipping something green and slushy. I'm
drinking beer. We're in a place called Breezes. Everything is on tap if you have a wristband on and the
wristband only enhances the sense that I've been
sectioned. I flash the wristband at the barman, but he
doesn't care anyway. He pulls another bottle out of
the ice bin, and the others all say they'll have one too.
Except Barry. No one knows what Barry wants.

'Where's Barry?' I ask.

Rich nods to the far side of the room. Barry is in
front of the band on the dance floor, arms in the air,
gyrating his hips in a Hieronymus-Bosch-meets-
Tony-Hadley-love-machine boogie, clearing the floor
like a minesweeper. It's the Garden of Earthly Angel
Delights.

'Let's go down.' Jim means to the underground
disco. We've done the pool, pina coladas in the
shallow end, marks out of ten for the passing

bottoms. We've done the topless observation sorties. We've done the eat-your-weight in banana fritters. Tape my eyes open in front of *Holby City*. Slam my todger in a fridge door. Anything but this – only the disco remains. My nightmare is young.

Sean is already wondering if the Chernobyl sisters are down there – a week's seminal hypertension waiting to unload, which is worrying since we are sharing a room. The general verdict on the Chernobyl sisters is that they look like drag queens, but Sean senses potential. We grab Barry from the dance floor. He follows willingly, but stops suddenly in the hall, turning his head fast after a passing girl. He throws his arm back and forth as she walks away down the corridor. He crouches. Everyone laughs, knowing the joke by now. 'Ten o'clock,' says Rich. Barry strips in invisible fly line. 'Going left. Going away, going away. Strip, strip. Oh hell. You've spooked her!'

The disco is a throbbing pit. Twenty by twenty (feet, not metres), the place reverberates like a jack-hammer. Faces hug the walls, and press in on the bar. The floor is empty. The Chernobyls are over by the far wall, but a local Lothario has already marked the prettiest down as an easy pull and is all over her. Sean sits on a stool looking for an opening. I get a beer and stand by the bar only to find myself bopping pathetically to the beat.

Barry hits the empty floor, and starts his 'Gold!' routine. He breaks the ice, and a few others join in. A foxy black girl starts up next to Barry. A wannabe disco king dancing to the mirrors shows Barry the way. The girl bends down, legs straight. The disco king funks up behind her, grabs one haunch, throws one arm high, and starts riding, and rubbing. His crotch presses her behind and she throws her head around in mock pleasure. Barry likes the look of this, thumps Disco King out of the way, and takes up the reins. He's good too. Disco King doesn't get a look-in. Barry is dancing for Queen and Country. The music is going . . .

> Don't blame it on the sunshine
> Don't blame it on the moonlight
> Don't blame it on the good times
> Blame it on the boogie

The same song that's been playing in my head since midweek. And now I know what it means! The whole week has been an atonement. Salvation doesn't respect the second law of thermodynamics, the arrow of time. It means we suffered before we sinned. It means that Breezes, Grand Bahama, might be hedonism on a plate, but hedonism has a price. We have paid the price. It was a week trying – and failing – to catch a bonefish, just one lousy bonefish, sandwiched between two hurricanes, isobars dropping like knickers at a car-key-and-fondue party in Solihull, under the examining light of a September full moon. All foretold, if only I'd known it, in the book of Michael Jackson. Owoooooooooooooooo.

Hurricane Cay

We arrive to find our rooms just in time before the light fades away in the western sky. I check my place over. Nice beach apartment, two floors, big bed, air conditioning going too hard. I look out the window, but it's dark already and I catch my own shagged-out after-travel reflection looking back at me. God knows how Barry feels. He emptied the bar on the plane. Maybe he's afraid of flying. On the other hand maybe he just likes drinking. I step outside on to the porch, and hear voices. Rich, Jim and Jason are under the palm trees by the shore, chatting and smoking. Waves slap against the coral shoreline. The palm trees are rustling in the breeze. 'The wind picked up an hour or two ago,' says Rich. 'Which would be about when we arrived.'

'That's usually how it works.' I look out to sea. The lights of New Exmouth shine brightly across the other side of the bay. The sea between is black like a cave. A warm, soft wind off the water stirs the trees again. Only a small patch of clear sky remains, high to the west, and the clouds around it catch the last orange glow of the sun. To our left a dock runs out into the bay.

'Can you stand this for a week?' asks Jason.

'Oh yes.'

After supper we come back here with a few bottles

of beer and sit on the dock. We chuck bait out and wait for whatever might pass by. I'm knackered, so I lie down on the dock, and feel it buffer and shake under me as the waves smack into the pillars. The air feels ominous. Once in a while a weak flash stirs across the sky to the east. The wind pushes the storm our way, and soon the flashes illuminate the sky right across the horizon.

'That will be the hurricane closing in then.'

'I thought it was going away,' I say.

'Looks like it's forgotten something.'

The wind picks up, but the night air is still sticky and close. Suddenly Jason's hand-line spool clatters across the boarding. He grabs it and yelps as the line cuts his fingers. The fish reaches the far end of the jetty, and stops, the line solid. I find my torch and shine a light down into the water. We think the fish is wrapped around the pier. It won't move. No one wants to get down there and unwrap the line. Jason decides to pull as hard as he can, and suddenly the beast breaks free and powers away from the dock, Jason cursing and holding on as tight as he can. The fish is impossible to move so Jason takes off his shoe, wraps the line around it and heaves back as hard as he can, walking back up the pier. Whatever is at the far end gives slowly until finally it arrives at the surface in a cross-beam of torchlight.

'Holy cow, it's a ray. It's massive. That is a massive ray.'

We have no idea how to deal with it. It's too far

down, it won't pull up, and no one wants to touch it. The ray hangs on the surface flapping gently, until someone says, 'We're gonna have to pull it up as far as we can and cut the line.' Jason heaves back again and the fish rises slowly, squirting water out of its mouth. As the full weight comes off the water the hook straightens, and the fish crashes back to the surface, much to everyone's relief. But the adventure is sharpened now by the appearance of this behemoth. As the lightning flicks up the clouds, and the wind whips across the sea, lines are cast again, everyone wondering what else might be out there. A few raindrops start to fall, and suddenly a fish jumps right in front of us. The white splash as it hits the water shines enormously and briefly in the dark. 'What the hell was that?' asks Sean.

'Probably a tarpon.' I cast to the spot but hope nothing takes.

'That's the thing about this dock,' says Rich. 'You never know what's out there. Anything could pass by. Anything.'

That night I slept on and off. Whenever I woke lightning was flickering outside, the fiery tail of the hurricane we passed through on our flight over. The storm missed Blue Crab Cay, but it had ruffled a few hairpieces on expensive yachts in the bay. September was a risky time to be here, but bonefish addicts don't look gift horses in the mouth – when Rich called and asked if I'd like to go fishing with a few of his mates and Jason from the Tourist Board, I just said yes I would. Besides, the hurricane was through now and with any luck hungry fish would come chomping up the line. I lay awake as the fan whirred over the bed and thought of the bonefish out there, hunting shrimp on the mangrove flats. The palm leaves outside flapped in the breeze. I bloody love bonefish country.

But in the morning the weather was grey, wet and windy. Awful bonefish weather.

The Best Worst Day

Don and his brother are both native Bahamians, both bonefish guides. I'm told some sort of rivalry exists between the two of them. They try not to talk to each other, though they will be civil enough in company. Some people say it's business. Some say it's a woman. All I hear of it on this first day is when we're trying to fix Don's engine – he says he is not going to go and get any parts off his brother, just in passing, as if I should know why not. Then later in the day he mentions his brother is getting all the business from the hotel, and how that is pissing him off.

Don is light and wiry, about five ten. He talks quietly, and it is difficult to hear his instructions when it's my turn up front. He calls me boss. His brown skin is dried by the sun. He wears flip-flops. He has a bonefish necklace – the gold fish nestles in the bleached white hairs of his chest. His back gives him trouble and in the end it shortens our day.

The first thing that went wrong was the engine started to misfire fifty yards away from the dock. Don let out a curse, and dropped the revs. He lifted the cover and fiddled with something. He revved it again, but it was still a problem. We trundled slowly over to a nearby boatyard to look for a spare plug. There was no one in.

One cylinder was misfiring. Don went through the routine of trying to isolate which one, but it took ages. He was getting increasingly agitated, running the boat out into the bay and back to the dock time and again, and each time the dogs on the pier got excited that he was coming back. He went in to fetch a few more plugs. We fiddled with the engine again, slipping one lead off at a time, and suddenly all three cylinders fired up, and the crackly half-beat turned into a mellow roar. Now Don had to get some fuel. We motored over to the fuelling dock, and Don shouted up. A huge woman came out of the shed. She handed Don the bowser and sat in front of us, her tie-dyed blue dress failing to conceal acres of white skin dimpled like the surface of the moon. Finally she waddled into the office to mark up Don's tab. She passed a sign that read THE WORST DAY FISHING BEATS THE BEST DAY WORKING.

We started the day at Harbour Flats, and saw a fish feeding head-down, half out of the water – tailing. Rich was on the front but the wind was up, and the light was difficult. It was gone before we got close.

We didn't even touch a fish poling in front of the town and the wrecker's yard. In the end Don dropped me on an empty beach while he took Rich further away down the island. I waded the line between the turtle grass and the sand. Someone came jogging along the beach with his dog. The dog chased birds off the beach, running after them, splashing through shallow water, until the birds were high and far away and obviously beyond reach, even to the dog. The dog ran back to its master wagging its tail. The guy jogged up and down for ages.

Suddenly I noticed a bonefish. I got two casts in before it moved away. I love the way bonefish move, with no visible motion of their fins, like they are sliding, like a slot car. This one picked up speed as it passed me and was gone. I start to see others, glinting in the sun as they turn to feed, or their shadows ghosting over the sand. One tails beside me. Another moves towards me as I'm changing the fly – when I can finally cast, he's too close, and shoots off as soon as my rod moves. Another lies motionless ahead of me as I cast at him again and again, until he too slips away.

The same happened again after lunch. This time I was back on the boat with Rich and Don. We drifted across the same flat, but were defeated by the wind, the light and my own lack of karma. Finally, I caught a fish out of a mudding shoal in the deeper water – as close as you can get with bonefishing to shooting a rat in a barrel. A bull of a fish, it ran three or four times, circled the boat and didn't give up. 'It tested the knots,' I said to Rich. It didn't count though. Not in my mind. I wanted to get back to the beach, to have another chance at those big fish on my own. But Don's back was killing him and so was his engine. We motored in early, firing on two cylinders.

Something Big

Dickie is different from Don. He's more confident, has a cleaner shirt, a cleaner boat and an engine that works. But the day proves as difficult. I put it down to the wind and light, neither of which is ideal, though I've caught bonefish before in bad wind and poor light.

I take a stand up front. Dickie is spotting fish I can't see and soon I begin to feel useless. Rich is anxious for me to catch something and anxious for me to have a good time. We pole from one spot to the next, the water a curtain of grey into which only Dickie can see. I don't catch or properly see a fish all morning. When I think about it I hate bonefishing from a boat. Fishing is largely about getting into the natural world on your own, and the more in touch you are the better. The insulation and social cauldron of a boat is a second-grade version of the sport. Plus Rich's anxiety – which may or may not be in my imagination – is making me tense. My casting is crap. I can't see the fish. After a few hours I can only think about that flat and the fish I missed yesterday. I'm itching to get back there. Overhead the sky is an unbroken field of grey. The wind freshens. 'Smells like something is brewing,' Dickie admits finally.

A house on the Rynda

Dusk over the Rynda

Fishing the upper Rynda

Casting for sea trout off a Norfolk beach

A big trout from the Year of the Big Fish

The Frome near Nine Hatches

Another big trout from the Year of the Big Fish

An Icelandic trout

Ronnie on the Upper Big Laxa

Blue Crab Quay

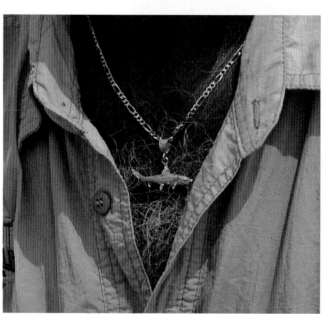

Bonefish
necklace

Signs

Barry moonbathing

A bonefish

A shoal of bonefish

'Are we sure the hurricane has gone away?' I ask. No one answers but a few minutes later we decide to give up on the bones we can't see and go chasing barracuda out on the reef. We run through a gap in the islands and out to the open sea. Rollers stand up over the rocks about a mile out. We turn inside here and run north, two fresh fish trolled out the back. The first hit pops the screws in the rod holder and nearly snaps the rod.

'Watch out! Watch out! Hell, that is a big fish!' I'm nearest, so I grab the rod and heave. It feels like the barracuda is off. The rod has no bend at all. It's a broomstick. Finally, we find a small fish on the end of the line.

'That's not the same fish,' says Rich. 'It can't be.' We run further, catch a second fish, then a third, each a little bigger than the last. It feels good bending the rod into something, riding the poling platform, watching the baits, waiting for a hit – but I'm not sure it's fishing.

I must have got that dreamy, faraway look on my face, because after a while Rich looked at me and suggested to Dickie they put me back at the beach.

They dropped me there and, with a wave, shot off round the headland to look for more barracuda and snappers. I stood still for a moment, scanning the horizon. I had a small patch of sun overhead and the white sand glared in the fresh light. Two hundred yards away, a stir in the water caught my eye. A bonefish. No, a shark. But it didn't move like a shark.

It came off the turtle grass, gliding. Beyond the fish the sun hit the water for half a mile, then a grey sheet of shadow began. The wind was stiff, and the patch of sun was moving quickly towards me. I reckoned I had a minute to get within casting range, and started to wade, my heart thumping. With every step I was more and more certain that it was a bonefish, the biggest bonefish I'd ever seen. The grey shadow that would turn the lights out was racing across the flats. I was going to lose. I was within forty yards when the steel curtain dropped, and the fish disappeared. It was a fifteen-pound bonefish. At least a fifteen-pound fish.

I stood still and waited. I looked north. There was no patch of sun on the way. After a moment I heard a stir on the water, and turned to my right to see this huge tail wave above the surface twenty feet from me. I made one cast. Nothing. I waited again. I waited until the sun arrived. When it did my fish was gone. It was the same for the rest of my hour on the flat: fish seen at a distance, gone by the time I got close enough to cast a fly, always swimming away.

Big Bitches
After supper I join the others back on the dock, though I'm having trouble keeping up with the drinking. Barry has hollow legs and Jim's got into a rum called 151. Barry has set himself up on a deck-chair, moonbathing. The moon is so bright it is casting shadows. He has a row of beer bottles beside

him and his rod is held at an angle that kind of implies an approaching encounter with a monster from the deep. Jim has caught some snapper, and is lobbing them out whole attached to a hand line. 'There are some big bitches out there,' he says, enigmatically.

Pirate Cay

'I don't usually swear,' said Dickie, 'but those fish are friggin' big. That one out there at the head of the shoal, that one would have lit your reel right up. It weighed eighteen pounds. Go left. Go right. Strip. Strip. Falling away. Too short. Damn. Those fish aren't seeing it. Another. 'Bout eleven o'clock. 'Bout a hundred feet. Damn. Let's go with a darker fly. They're all over this flat. All over it. They've got my panties tied right up in a knot.'

Rich spotted one. 'We've got a big boy coming in off the side.' Dickie spotted it too. It was my turn to cast.

'Three of them coming at ya, Charles. Twelve o'clock. Fifty feet. Strip. See him? Strip. Strip. No, too short. Son of a bitch!'

Pirate Cay is a small island to the north of Blue Crab, only a few minutes by boat. The flat is off a sandy beach stretching west behind the island. The gentlest of surfs curls in around the point and washes in across the sand. I can hear a cock crowing above the noise of the waves. 'If these fish were feeding we'd have a ball.'

'Yep. Well, don't despair, Rich. We'll get one.'

'I'm not despairing. Can't think of anywhere I'd rather be.'

'Well, come on now. That ain't hard.' Dickie pushes on the punt pole. 'I'd rather be on a beach with a naked chick, margarita in my hand.'

We pole around the cay for a while longer, Dickie in a margarita-and-naked-chick reverie, Rich and me taking it in turns to spook big bonefish by showing them flies, and speculating in between about what's making them so finicky. Rich thinks it's the hurricane, the weather fronts sweeping in. 'We arrived at the tail end of one hurricane, and now there's another brewing over Cuba. They can't like this pressure dropping so fast.'

Dickie thinks it's the full moon. 'That moon was so bright last night. These fish could have been feeding for hours. Maybe they just ain't hungry. That moon is not on our side.'

I'm listening to the two of them swap theories with a disco hit playing in my head – 'Don't blame it on the sunshine / Don't blame it on the moonlight / Don't blame it on the good times . . .' 'I think it's the boogie,' I say. 'Blame it on the boogie.'

'I like your thinking, Charles,' said Dickie. 'Blame it on the boogie.' At the top end of the island, on Dickie's banker, the flat he'd been telling us about all morning, the one always full of fish – we found nothing. Well, I found nothing. Rich bumped into a shoal round the first corner and pulled an eight-pound fish out of it. I heard the splashing beyond a line of mangroves and tried not to notice. I was feeling like an idiot, desperate to catch one of these wretched fish not only for the sake of it, but to convince Rich that I could do it, that I was enjoying myself, that I'd go home with something to write about.

The water feels like a bath, and in this still lagoon the noon heat builds like a pressure cooker. I walk slowly up a creek in the mangroves, lifting my feet like a wading egret. I have the light with me and if there's a fish in here I'll see it. I go to the top end and stand still. I can hear a boat running its engine on the far side of the mangroves, a faint gurgling noise. The boat pulls away and leaves me in silence. It's so quiet I could hear a fish, if only one were here. I wait twenty minutes, occasionally crouching low to look along the flat water for the slightest sign of movement. The others are wading around in circles, looking like strange storks in a swamp. They aren't casting. I call over. They've seen nothing.

We stopped by Pirate Cay again on the way back and rocked in the gentle swell examining the bay for signs of fish. The shoal had gone, but Dickie saw a big bonefish cruising the very edge of the beach in skinny water. I had to get out to follow, but it was swimming away from me just out of range and I was moving as quickly as I could go without splashing. I tried a few casts but they fell short. When the fish finally turned at the apex of the beach by a stand of dried and bleached mangroves I could hear my heart pounding.

I put out a cast without spooking the fish. The fly settled. The fish came forward. One pull. Then another. The fish saw the fly and came right at it, with such intent I started to shake and my right eye started to twitch. I was wired like a bomb. My cheek muscles started to jigger up and down. Hell! I was probably sending all this bad karma down the line. The bonefish pulled up behind the fly, took one look, then overtook it, like the fly was a car in the slow lane. The fish swam on, past me, speeding just a little and left the flat. In no sense was it spooked. It just wasn't hanging around. What can I do?

Sundowner's

The sky breaks wide open with white lightning flashing right down to the sea – the new hurricane must be closing in. It's our last night but one. We head over to New Exmouth for a few more drinks – I think Barry and Jim have emptied the bar at the hotel. It's no time to take a boat. In my solitary sobriety I suggest golf carts, but the suggestion gets drowned in a chorus of piratical oaths as everyone climbs aboard an unseaworthy dinghy. They paddle off into the dark – singing – and I take the cart option, wondering what does happen when lightning hits the sea you're floating in. For all I know they're in a Faraday cage, and this buzzing electric motor under me is a come-on for lightning. I may fry while they drink. On the other hand, of course, they may fry, then drown.

But they are there when my golf cart finally

wheezes into town. The storm is still flirting with the island, flaring electric light over the tables and dock outside Sundowner's, where Barry is already in competition with the local dude drinking hero, and the island's own brand of Tequila Slammer, the Tequila Stuntman – snorting salt up his nose, drinking enormous shots in one hit, and squeezing lime into his eye. You know, I really don't think I'll join in on this. Even Jim shies away from the task. Behind the bar a blackboard lists the names of the record holders, and Barry is determined to get to the top of it. The dude is egging him on – unnecessarily. The rest of us stick to Kalik lager, play pool and watch the spectacle unfold. The storm adds a Hammer House tone to the bacchanalian scene. Barry creeps further up the leader board with every drained glass. He's arm in arm with the dude, swaying and swearing and laughing his way into New Exmouth's record books. His nose is bright red, one eye is half closed and he's wobbling a lot. Only when finally he tops the chart, having downed biblical amounts of Tequila, does the dude let on the list is for Slammers consumed in a week not one night.

Good to Be Alone
It's great to fish alone. In the end that is why I do it – for the solitude.

On the final day I hung around my room for a while, then went for a swim off the short beach by the dock we fished off in the evenings. The others had gone back out to sea after barracuda. I'd negotiated a day without guides – a day by myself with a golf cart to get me to Harbour Flats, round the far side of the bay. I had some unfinished business with those enormous bonefish. Before leaving, I swam up and down the beach a few times, looking for shrimp and crab along the line between the turtle grass and the sand, for signs of what the bonefish might be eating. As I stood on the beach drying myself a dark shape appeared, swimming towards me head on. A big bonefish! I rushed to the palm tree I had left my rod under, but by the time I'd got the fly out, the fish was gone. I paced the beach for twenty minutes trying to find it again.

I found the golf cart and drove to New Exmouth, along the narrow, furrowed dirt lanes of the island, taking the wrong turn more than once in a maze of tracks and driveways leading to development plots. Along the east side of the island the road skirted the Atlantic coast – a narrow strip of sand, fringed with wind-blown trees, dropping quickly into the deep blue of the ocean, and buffeted by heavy, fat waves rolling steeply up and over, grabbing at the beach. I bought grouper and fries at a harbourside café, splashed chilli sauce on the grouper, drank a beer and took my time, until I guessed the tide was right.

I have a hand-drawn map to get to Harbour Flats, but like all hand-drawn maps sketched late in the evening it makes no sense at all. I can't find any way through the thick scrub from the road to the flats and eventually I have to drive back out of town along a track that ends at a beach on the east side of the island, then walk a mile or so to the point of the island and round the top to the west side. I'm pleased I bother though, because at the northern tip, on the Atlantic side but sheltered by another island, I find bonefish fading in and out of the milky water, gliding off the turtle grass, across the sand and out of sight again. I get some good casts in too, the fly a few feet – even yards – in front, waiting for the fish. The fish keep coming – they are swimming along the surf line. But every time I move the fly they turn away. I've never seen such big bonefish.

A storm-shower comes up from behind and catches me in the open on the beach. The rain is ripe, warm and heavy, thumps craters into the sand and soaks my shirt. All my stuff, including a camera, is in a rucksack lying open a couple of hundred yards away. The only shelter is in some scrub on the point. I grab my rucksack and in bare feet run into the scrub, picking up burrs that look like the top end of medieval maces. When the shower passes I go back to the beach and the bonefish are still there. I try again until they melt away.

Around the point in the still water on the west side I find hundreds more – tailing, stirring up mud, drifting along the shoreline in twos and threes, or running in big shoals across the black weed and white sand, chameleoning from dark to light again as they go. The plink of a fly with bead-chain eyes scatters the fish as much as fifteen yards away. I switch to an unweighted fly, but it is no better. The fish are simply impossible. Once in a while I get a follow or a pair of fish runnning down the fly like cats, but they always turn away. Always.

Two neatly attired . . . well, they must be Americans by the look of them . . . show up, all in white, wading belts, flats boots, bleach-white caps and big cigars. As they walk along the beach one of them stops suddenly, crouches and points. His friend puts out a cast. The fly lands and the water explodes with spooked fish. I shout over that they're going to need hand grenades and get a friendly wave back. They fish behind me a few hundred yards up the flat towards New Exmouth. In the next two hours I see a lot of crouching, pointing, casting and fly-box examination, but I don't see any catching.

A fresh storm rides over the top of the island, a stroppy plate thrown out of the hurricane's kitchen, though out here we are on the edge of it. The main bulk of clouds is to the east but in the west they're darkening the sky to the horizon. I see flashes of lightning to the west. Then a streak to the east. Fifteen seconds later a rip of thunder. Rain draws towards me across the water, a crescendo of fizzing, overhead now.

Suddenly the view to the surrounding islands is gone. Outlines blur. The Americans disappear behind a curtain of rain. Overhead the clouds are black, but the sky behind is clear. The rain peels away south and west. The water stops fizzing. It is completely quiet. A swirl in the water brings me back to the moment. A big silver tail waves over a dark, billowing cloud of mud. I go back to the fish. I always go back to the fish.

Paradise Found

THE LAGOON IS FLAT. A GENTLE RIPPLE LAPS AGAINST the white sand at my feet, creating a clicking noise as water fills dry holes. Imperceptibly the water seeps in, flooding over the young coral at the edge of the sand. Ten feet out mullet suck and swirl at the surface. Beyond, a slight swell spends itself on a reef at the edge of the lagoon, a soft rush – the waves ending their journey by water, but continuing as sound.

The narrow, dusky white beach is bordered by mangroves. Fallen palm trees, stripped and bleached, reach out over the water. I run my feet back and forth across the sand, entranced by the soft pulsing of the sea. The sky is light blue overhead, fading paler above a bank of clouds stretched along the horizon. The clouds are another wave, an echo of the sea. The trailing edge of a storm that never happened, rolling out to the east, leaving this clear sky behind it.

Small crabs wait at the edge of holes in the sand, half in, half out. I count five of them. I move and the crabs scurry inside. The high cirrus clouds which made the sky a pale blue minutes ago have turned pink, and suddenly a full moon is shining strongly against the fading daylight. In the gathering dark I can just make out a heron, hunting by moonlight.

The weather report in the bar said our cyclone was moving away. The sky has cleared and the moon shines off the top ridge of surf, like a tear in black cloth. The waves rumble in, soft and endless. I can't even locate the part of me that came here nerve-racked and stressed out by the endless chatter and displacement activity of life-in-the-machine. It's gone. I drop my head back, and make an angel in the sand, fanning my arms up and down. I've got six more days of this.

We had weird weather all day. The cyclone, Vaughan told us, was big enough to have a name, though no one knew what it was. I saw the shape of it on the satellite map the other fishing party had at breakfast. They drank coffee with long faces while the map lay on the table between them. One of the group took the time to show me where on the circulating mass of red our small atoll lay. Under a feeder, not even the main cyclone which lay two hundred miles to the south-west, not moving, just throwing out squally weather fronts, one of which had passed through in the night, another of which was rattling the palm trees right then, ripping cool air across the breakfast table. There was a spit of rain but it stopped quickly. I stepped on to the beach to look at the sky. All around were dark clouds, and veils of rain hanging heavily beneath them. Out on the reef big rollers blocked the horizon, turning it into a roiling blue line. When the wind turned or dropped I heard the waves.

Three days from home, I'm itching to get into a fish and this awful weather has made me miserable. I wonder whether it is even worth bothering. But when I get to the beach where the boats are, Andrew and Vaughan are set to go. Andrew says something about it being the worst day of weather we have had all season, but beyond that he seems far more concerned about a freighter ship trying to dock near his boat.

'He's a complete friggin' idiot. He hasn't got a clue what he's doing.' The rusted hulk moves out into the bay to come round for one more try. Vaughan decides to load and get going quickly before the ship returns.

Beyond the lagoon those big blue rollers break remorselessly, rearing up as inky walls, dissolving in explosions of white foam, unzipping back and forth across the reef. A gap appears where the waves peel through, exaggerated and unbroken, before dissipating into the expanse of the lagoon. The swell pitches our boat violently. I turn to see how Vaughan is doing. He is riding a tiny flats skiff back to the fishing ground. His boat leaves the water at the crest of the wave, and I see the propellor spinning in the air before the skiff crashes back into the next trough. Out to sea the rough water slackens, though dark currents still swirl menacingly below the boat. It seems insane even to think about fishing today.

But once across the channel and inside St François the swell dies, and bizarrely the wind drops too, as if it, like the waves, has crashed and died on the surrounding reefs. St François is a horseshoe-shaped atoll, ten thousand acres, divided into kidney lagoons at its centre, each accessed by only one or two narrow channels. At the southern end is the island of the same name, a smaller mirror image of the surrounding reef and flats. To the west is Bijoutier, just a crown of sand, coconut trees and a few birds. The tide is running out, and within a few hours the full expanse of the flats will be exposed, white sand shimmering to the horizon, at its outer edge the coral reef.

We started fishing in a heavy shower, the wind at our backs, the flats underwater, but the tide running off quickly, seeping off the crowns of sand into a maze of channels where the water showed blue-green against the yellow of the shallows. We walked downwind with only a small window of vision through the glare of dull light. A grey shape moved, cutting an angle from the deeper channel across a sandbar and back, switching in and out of sight, lost in reflections and over patches of turtle grass which stain the sandy flats with feathery blankets of dull green. I put a fly across its path. Too close. Without hurrying the fish slips back into deeper water. Bones shift without effort, a transition across sand.

Other fish followed. I led one well, let the fly settle then twitched it. The fish turned and went quickly to the fly, following along the sand until it stopped and tipped up on the fulcrum of its snout. I love the way bonefish pounce on a fly, like a cat chasing a ball on a string. I pulled to set the hook but he didn't quite have it. I pulled again, and the fish followed one more time, faster now, determined to get that sucker. I tried to set the hook with one long drag on the line. The fish swam at me shaking its head. I tightened the line to catch him, but missed and he spat the fly.

There are fish everywhere. I can see a pair mooching slowly round the circumference of a shallow bay, and then, closer, a movement catches my eye. A bonefish zips off the turtle grass across the sand and away into the deep like a bobsleigh. The pair of fish are nearer now and beyond them a shoal is moving straight at me, half a dozen grey hulls against the green grass pushing a delicate bow wave ahead. They pause and converge on the same spot. There is a flurry in the water, then they fan out again and keep on coming, right at me.

I make a decision and cast, just as one fish turns, followed by the other. They miss my fly and when they turn back they are too close. I freeze. Slowly I roll the rod into another cast. The line follows, lifting the fly high in the air, landing it with a clumsy plop. But the fish don't spook. One of them sees my fly as soon as I move it and reduces the distance between us by half. It's right under me now. I can pick out its scales, and the dome of fluid over its eyes. I stop breathing. If my shoe so much as crunches a grain of sand the fish will scram. The fish swims right up to the fly, stops but doesn't tip. I move the fly again but snag it over a piece of coral. I can hear my heart now, thumping hard. The fish is under the rod. The rod is shaking.

The bonefish tries to pick the fly up. Shakes its head because the fly is stuck. I strip the line hard, but it's solid on the coral. The bonefish sees my arm move, feels the fly, and fires off from under me, a whorl of disturbed sand tracing out behind. The line picks up, sucks across the surface, then snaps the rod down. The rod is pointing now at the fading tracer of sand, then a white shape streaking over turtle grass, still running the line down, the reel shrieking hard until the running slows. Then the fish takes the line in pulses, pumping into the greyer, deeper water under that massive bank of clouds building over us.

I have the bonefish suspended across the palm of my right hand. It's three inches across the shoulders. Its head hangs down slightly, the mouth drooping open, but so inert, so contained. I turn to Vaughan who's been behind me all along. 'This, Vaughan, is a cosmic mind-fuck of note. I've never seen so many bonefish.'

'Not bad, hey? Not bad to catch a bone before eight thirty. You haven't seen anything yet, man. This is a warm-up lap. That's all.'

All around the horizon squalls and fronts beat across the Indian Ocean. At two in the afternoon the clouds darkened above us, swelling up behind St

François, a deep blue blurring the line between sea and sky, rain in a gauze at its edges. It towered overhead. But the rain never came, and the front peeled away to the east. I caught a lot of bonefish. More than I cared to count. One was taken by a shark. A few came off on coral. I sat on the nose of the skiff, and said to Vaughan I'd hate to think what the place was like with good weather.

Andrew had other fish on his mind. It was his day off from guiding, but he was back where he spends the other six days of the week, looking for an appointment with a giant trevally – the gangster of the flats. We could see Andrew now, over a mile away, on the far side of St François. He was sitting on the casting platform at the back of his skiff waiting for this one enormous trevally to hunt through the channel in front of his boat. 'Has he been there since this morning?' I asked.

'All day. He's just waiting for this one fish. It's a bus, though. A real bus. He'll see it a mile off if it goes through there.' We chatted on, eating sandwiches, draining the big bottle of iced water. I thought I saw movement on Andrew's skiff. He stood up for a moment, high on the platform, then dropped out of sight.

'Andrew looked like he was casting just now.'

'I'll see how he's getting on.'

Vaughan crackled his walkie-talkie into life. 'Yo, Andrew. Any action?'

We heard nothing for a moment, then a voice crackled back. Andrew sounded urgent. I couldn't tell what he was saying. 'What's up, Vaughan?'

'Andrew's into it. That means it's the big one. We better get down there.' We buzzed across the flats. The tide had turned again, drowning the yellow fingers of sand. We ran right over them to shorten the journey. The deep blue of the twisting channels curved back and forth under us as we flashed across the surface.

'He's still into it.' I could see that Andrew's rod was bent right over. He was on the nose of the skiff, the rod point hard against the water. Vaughan dropped the throttle back and we coasted in. Andrew's rod bucked, and line jumped off the reel in bursts, like he was hooked to some boulder rolling down the reef to the sea floor. Vaughan jumped over into Andrew's skiff, and stood waiting. Slowly Andrew stole back line, though the trevally kept turning. Our boats circled gently in the still water. None of us said a word. It was hot. Andrew grunted and his feet squeaked on the skiff deck as he fought for leverage. His reel rasped out line, clicking on its ratchet. The fish was deep and really powerful. A force of nature more than a fish. We stared into the water for ages, trying to get a look at it.

'A big one, hey?' said Vaughan.

'I haven't seen it since I hooked it.'

But Andrew was winning back line, winching, dragging the fish to the surface. A broad pewter back broke the top, and lunged again for the shade of the boat. Vaughan was suddenly flat on the deck, his arm over the side in a shower of spray. He had grabbed the trevally's tail and hauled the fish aboard. It was massive. Two and a half, maybe three feet long. The head alone was the size of a dustbin lid.

We motored to the nearest flat to weigh it. Andrew got the grips on its jaw but it bottomed-out the scale. 'It's over forty anyway,' said Andrew, shrugging.

The head of a trevally rises up in a steep curve from its enormous mouth. Two dark eyes – tilted forward for hunting – form the centre of the arc of forehead, which rides smooth and shiny into a high back over slab sides. The back end, though, looks to be glued on from a smaller model. A parts-bin fish out of the water, and yet so effortlessly aggressive and perfect in its element. Andrew held it for a few more pictures, then eased the fish upright into the deeper water at the edge of the flat. It swam away into the lagoon.

Tuesday dawned blue. I showered outside, cycled to breakfast, and then on to the dock slaloming the land crabs and falling coconuts. We were on the flats by eight, into bonefish by five past. The sky stayed blue, and at times the sea was grey with bonefish. Phalanxes of them came swimming towards us down the 'gravy train' channel, in shoals of fifty, or a hundred. Masses of them, with the bigger fish in ones and twos. That night when I closed my eyes I saw a shimmering sandflat with bonefish moving across it.

The place was burnt into my retina. I had caught so many I told Vaughan we'd only go for the big fish from now on. He laughed and said he'd take me over to the ocean side – it was his medicine for saturated appetites. He meant the outside of the reef, a rocky and desolate shoreline I was surprised would even hold bonefish. The bones over there were a different thing altogether, he said. I ought to try the triggerfish too. Vaughan said everyone he fished with had given up on bones once they'd hooked a triggerfish.

I hooked a small one early that day, and the fish took off for the reef edge with speed and grinding power out of all proportion to its size. Physics gave way to Looney Tunes. I was connected to some cartoon freak, waiting for a dumb-bell to fall on my head, a fish to fire itself from a cannon marked Acme or a hole to open in the sea, a grinning swordfish sawing a perfect circle around me. The little fish broke the line, and the rest of the day was lost.

I saw a good one pirouette in a wave. They hang, nose down, big blowsy tails wafting in the current like knickerbockers on the line. He rolled, his nose glued to the same spot, dragging a crab out of a hole in the coral. Pulling at it, moving back and forth in the water like a dog wrestling a slipper. I put a cast nearby to get his attention. Left, right; it's a lottery with a triggerfish, as they rotate haphazardly. The first cast was behind his belly – a blind spot because a triggerfish has a very big belly. The second cast was just right. His fins flickered offbeat. 'What's this?

Ooh, I say, a handsome crab. Monsieur, you are spoiling us with these crabs.' The trigger ambled over like Reginald Scoff at a canapés party, dragging his fat belly across the floor, no problem with body image. Very few of the fish we saw had followed. One or two looked then turned away. But most of them had spooked on the cast, or when they saw the fly. I was ready for this fish to scram. But up went the tail, knock, knock went the line. Vaughan told me to wait for a solid pull. I could feel the fish chewing the fly. 'He won't even notice the hook,' said Vaughan. 'You should see his teeth.'

Suddenly the line pulled away. I drew back hard. The trigger morphed. The idle salad-dodger we'd cast to was now a bug-eyed Sprite with fins, in fourth gear, looking for the redline. The fish was gone. I saw smoke come out of the water. 'He'll go for the reef edge. That's where he's heading. You've got thirty yards . . . twenty . . . ten. Turn that sucker before he gets there. Turn that sucker or you're smoked. Jeez, that's a big trigger. Twelve pounds. He's a bus. You're smoked. He's there, man. He's gone.' I had the drag up full but the triggerfish just kept going, over the reef edge, then nothing. The line dropped dead. I reeled in. He'd chewed the Gamakatsu hook into a circle. Later I tried to do the same thing with a pair of pliers. I couldn't.

There are three types of trigger: Blue Margin, Yellow Margin, and Picasso. But the Yellow Margins are impossible, and the Picassos are hard to find. I was going to be happy just catching one. Triggerfish melt in and out of sight, evaporate, materialise somewhere else. They're tricky to see – unless they're feeding in shallow water when their tails wave above the surface – and easy to lose. Sometimes we'd see their amber flanks, or a white belly as they rolled around, but then the fish would vanish, though I never took my eyes off the spot. The crab had to be just so, and never the same twice.

More refusals, evaporations and spookings followed, until at last we found a trigger feeding intently. He followed my fly three times, turning away each time to chew on something more interesting. Finally we switched to a merkin crab, and he moved four feet to take it first time. I pulled the hook home, and he set off like the last fish, straight for the coral heads at the far side of the lagoon. The reef edge was further away, and this time I turned him, though I had to pull so hard I thought the line would surely break. He grunted like a baby pig when I finally dragged him up across the turtle grass, and spat water at me when I lifted him to remove the hook. A crazy fish: a fat, distended belly, a stream-lined triangular face with eyes like the headlights on a Citroën 2CV and teeth like steel plates, three powerful fins at the back end, and sickle spikes top and bottom, anchors for holes in the coral. My one was seven pounds on the nose. A good size, but small compared to the bus.

* * *

The days roll past, a routine of two big bonefish to walk off breakfast, and then trigger-hunting. Trevally if we see them. It's hard to imagine fishing any better than this. But we haven't yet tried for a milkfish. Milkfish are folklore. An air of secrecy surrounds them, and they don't actually feed on anything you can represent with a fly. Everyone is sceptical, including the competing fishing tour operator, who feels the whole business might be hokum. One night I bring up the subject of milkfish in his company over drinks. He gets quite animated about the fact that it's all bullshit, though his rods want to find out whatever it is I know, and I feel sure I've just stepped on a viper's nest of rivalry.

Mostly, though, I'm on my own with a beer and a book called *Dirty Havana Trilogy* by Pedro Juan Gutierrez, a Cuban poet. I picked the book up in the airport because I liked the cover and I was in a hurry. In the evenings I revisit the edge of the lagoon and read as the sun goes down, while the crickets sing their scratchy jangle. Pedro Juan writes frankly about his life in Havana, a life of subsistence and survival and sex. It is brilliant. The book and this pure landscape conspire to put me somewhere truly uplifting. But I know I've got no chance of holding on to that place. As soon as I hit the adverts and consumerism, and the brainwashed whirligig of need and reason, it will fall away like the drying fish scales flaking off the handle of my fly rod.

*   *   *

Vaughan's co-guide Arno knows about the milkfish. There are pictures of him holding them up all over the guides' hut. He's secretive about what fly he uses, and where he goes. But I've been told that if I don't ask about it too much he will be ready with an invite when the time is right. By Thursday Arno's channel is full of them. We get a call on the radio – in code because it's a public frequency – and leave the trigger-fish for another day.

The channel links one lagoon with another, and when we get there the tide is running through it. A shoal of seventy to a hundred milkfish mill about in the cut at the head of the channel, waiting, moving randomly. Arno is anchored up on one side, not too bothered to cast just yet. He's waiting too. We anchor opposite and sit in the sun. Waiting. The fish are huge. There is nothing smaller than fifteen pounds; some are easily over thirty. A big fish moves up to the top and spears across the surface. Its forked tail contracts down as it accelerates, then opens again when it turns and rejoins the shoal. Another fish does the same. The restless and random movement slowly conforms into a line of fish, breaks then forms again, until at some invisible signal of tidal pressure they line up again to swim up and down the channel, and the shoal becomes a circle. Arno stands at this and signals for me to start. Vaughan shows me the fly. It is no more than a green ball of floss. He tells me to cast it to intercept a feeding fish. If the hook drops to the right depth a fish may take it for the loose weed they're feeding on. It took ten minutes. Maybe twenty. Like fishing upriver with a nymph, I saw the leader move with the fish.

Vaughan knew straight away and was right behind with a hand on my shoulder to stop me striking. 'Don't do anything till I get the motor started.' I slacked the line for the seconds it took Vaughan to throw the anchor and start the engine. The fish swam on with the shoal. My heartbeat shook the rod. Vaughan was at the back of the boat lifting the anchor as quickly as he could. Then I heard the motor cough and start. He gunned the engine and shouted, 'Right, now hit it!'

I drew back hard on the line, and the fly reel took off, zero to 10,000 rpm in about half a second. Way, way faster than any bonefish. Within seconds the milkfish left the channel, travelling deep into the lagoon to my right, then turned and came right back past me and through to the other lagoon, my fly line lost in the curve, still trailing in one lagoon when the fish had reached the other. Suddenly the line fizzed past, chasing a white trail across the water, chasing my fish. 'Hold on. We've got to catch him or he'll spool you.'

I stood on the casting deck of the skiff, my fly rod held high, the reel still spinning crazily, though we were now chasing the fish under power. The milkfish was heading straight across the lagoon, nearly at the far side now, nearly at the finger flats. If it crossed those we'd never keep up. Vaughan had us at full throttle, until we came side on to the fish, and suddenly it sounded, pulling down as hard as it could, trying to reach the coral bed. I was lifting a rock off the floor, straining at the line.

We drifted under the hot sun. I swapped arms, moved the rod to change the pressure point, wondered if I could reach for some water. We drifted and the fish pulled. My rod was too weak. A nine-weight designed for bonefish, this nautilus had it curved into a hoop and I couldn't move. Forty minutes in the milkfish surged and broke the line. I can't say I ever saw the fish properly. Vaughan said that it had weighed about twenty-five pounds.

On the last day I have a thirty-minute window. The tide won't push until three, and I need to hook a fish early on to stand any chance of landing it by four – the time boats are supposed to leave St François. Arno has told me not to mess around so much, to give the fish some stick, get it on to a tight leash and hold it. It's the only way to land them. But his channel is empty. We sit and we wait. It's too late to go any-where else. No milk today. Then at half past a pod of only seven fish comes in. I cast to them before they form up, thinking, hoping one might turn on the fly. But they swim past over and over again, oblivious. I'm hanging my shoulders, on the edge of giving up, when suddenly they start to daisy-chain in the channel. One fish is much bigger than the others. It's my last shot and I concentrate on getting my fly right in front of it. I get a take. I can see my line move sideways. The milkfish continues with the shoal while Vaughan gets the boat ready. Then as the engine fires the hooked fish wakes up, bolts, feels the line then runs straight out of the channel, circles again just like yesterday's fish and runs back through, leaving me reeling crazily at all the slack line. But I'm still connected as the fish heads out into the lagoon, running fast against the drag. I turn the drag up hard and we close on the fish quickly. The milkfish leaps high out of the water, and dumps back into it with a huge splash. 'It's a bruiser, man. A bus! It's the big one,' Vaughan is shouting from the back.

'We've got to keep the fish tight to the boat. We can't let him sound.' I strain at the fish as hard as I can, pulling it sideways and backwards. Every time the fish changes direction I turn the rod and pull the other way. I have the fish on fifteen feet of line and don't let it take another inch. It swims back and forth, working for every beat of its tail. The enormous milk-fish is aboard in twenty minutes. I can't believe it. It's an extremity beyond a week of extremities. Vaughan and Andrew throw me high-fives, and start singing 'I'm a Believer'. They call me the milkman. Arno pats me on the back and says, 'That's the way to do it, man. You've got to give them bullets. You've got to make them cough. Cough medicine, man. No mercy.'

Back at Mahé I have a day to fill waiting for the plane home. I find an unpopular beach by a run-down bar

near the airport. No one is here except for a lady
mopping the floor and a fisherman repairing his boat
on the flats beyond the beach. The lady stops
mopping to get me a Coke on ice. I lie there all day
with my book, getting up once in a while to swim or
explore the rock pools for fish. When the sun gets low
and I have to think about leaving I ask the lady if
she'll call me a taxi. It arrives too soon. It's hard to
leave. But I've finished the *Trilogy*, and the beach is
buried in shade. The check-in hall seems so busy. And
leaking out of the ceiling all through the hall piped
music drips from fizzy speakers. It's an awful noise
after a week of silence. I can't get away from it,
though. It's in the café, the toilets, even out the front.
Finally I decide to go through to the departure
lounge. There is no music there. Instead, on a dozen
TV screens, in every corner, Jeremy Clarkson is over-
steering a Porsche 911 round an airfield. I never miss
a show back home. I hanker after a 911. But today it
seems to be exactly what I'd got away from all week
– it seems slightly obscene. Bloody hell. I really am
going home.

Now I'm at the end of another awful November afternoon, drizzling time away, failing to write anything,
looking out the window. The wind is picking up,
chasing in a bank of clouds that rears over the fields
behind like an impossibly massive wave. A wave of
sorts, I suppose, though not the warm swell of
Alphonse and St François. The air dampens, and my

map on the wall has buckled with the moisture. Yellow and white lights on the industrial estate blink on and off. Life is short and I'm wondering what the hell I live here for. I'm sure the schools are good on Mahé. And some of those islands have never been fished.

Letters Home from a Brazilian TV Adventure

Manaus, 10 January

WELL, WE GOT HERE.

I missed catching sight of Manaus as we landed. John told me how incongruous it looks from the air, a sprawling city completely surrounded by the impenetrable green of the jungle. Now at ground level I feel we could be anywhere in the tropics – only the city is steaming with the breath of the forest.

It will be a couple of days now before we can get out there. I feel like the Marlow character in *Apocalypse Now* stuck in a sweaty hotel room waiting to go into the dark heart of the jungle. Our plan is out the window. The rain has been pissing it down for weeks and the camp has cancelled on us. Apparently the river up there is all over the place, way out of its banks and into the jungle.

We filmed in Armando's bar this evening, near the opera house, me having a beer with Ivano.

Ivano is great – a real Latin force of nature. We sat at a table outside on the street. A soft-porn movie was playing on the TV in the bar, but we had to ask the owner to turn the sound down: the background moaning was getting in the way. I asked Ivano about the opera house. Turns out he also thinks opera is dull, which was a huge relief as up until then I had been feigning an interest in the whole thing. 'Yes, Charlie, I have to say I hate it all. It is rubbish.' I will get on well with Ivano!

Later, two drunks got into a fight and rolled off down the street behind us. I thought the drunks probably made better TV than me. It is hard to be comfortable with the camera. I've tried to imagine it's you listening to me, but in the end I'm talking to a machine and I feel a little unhinged.

You'll probably want to know what Manaus is like. The city rolls up and down as it sprawls towards the fringes of the rainforest, and in each dip grey, putrid streams flow energetically through all this colour. Houses are built up on stilts along the rivers. Those at the very edge stand over undercut banks and look as if they may fall in at the next flood. There's rubbish piled up under the houses – like geological strata of shredded plastic. Everything seems to be reused, recycled – except the plastic and cloth that litter the riverbanks like bunting. We passed piles of reclaimed car seats, shops full of old and busted-

Andrew with his enormous giant trevally

A triggerfish

Arno giving bullets
to a milkfish

Vaughan casting on
the St François flats

A bonefish from
Alphonse

Driving through Manaus

The Manaus fish market

An Amazon sunset

William at Woodmill Pool

A Bhutanese mural of a
spring-fed river

A sleeping dog in Thimpu

The Gangte Chhu

Palden at prayer

Young monks

Big Ben and his tope

up fridges and cookers, a store full of car-body panels neatly stacked behind a mesh fence.

We stopped at a bridge and Nathan pulled out the camera. A busty black lady wearing only a bra came to the window of her shack over the river to wring out a shirt. Nathan scanned the camera across the ramshackle buildings. She looked up blankly at us and the camera: used to being gawped at or filmed or photographed. Ivano says the people in these riverside *favelas* have come in from the jungle looking for work and have nowhere else to go. The *favelas* stretch along the flood plains, clinging to the land that no one and nothing wants, except from time to time, I suppose, the sewage-filled river.

My room is fine. A few mossies. The shower dribbles, but in Sam's room it delivers electric shocks. We've got to get up really early but I can't sleep. I'm lying here thinking about where a journey begins. Like the river, the story is now all over the place, so we have to film arse forwards – the end before the beginning.

11 January

I've stolen a minute while we're waiting at the front of the hotel for our van. It's 4 a.m. and we're off to film the fish market. The morning is a collage of noises. Our van has pulled up now with 'How Can We Let It Drift Away?' playing on the radio and its gentle, keys-in-the-ignition bong underlies the scratching of cicadas, a dog barking incessantly half a mile away, a cock crowing – he's a long way ahead of the dawn! Maybe we woke him. The others are loading enormous amounts of film gear into the van. I'd better lend a hand.

The market was frantic, a jostle of cars under spotlights, piles of bananas by the car park, muscle-bound men, squat under the weight of boxes or sacks of fish, pushing through the crowd. Melting iced water dripping down their backs, soaking their clothes as they climb the hill.

John wanted Nathan to film me walking through the crowd, looking at all the fish with Ivano. I had to ask around for peacock bass. The idea is that the local fishermen will know where to find them. The market is fascinating – weird fish of all kinds, but there's only one pile of small peacocks or *tucunaré* as they call them here. I asked. They've come from a long way away. In fact, I can see they have been frozen. The fisherman goes on to tell me the river is far too high here, and so it is impossible to find *tucunaré* at the moment. A few other fishermen say the same thing. The rain has blown out the whole Rio Negro. I think we are going to struggle to catch our fish.

At lunch we ate the fish and rice I'd just learnt to cook in Fatima's café. Some small shoeshine kids came up and asked if they could finish what

we hadn't eaten. We sent a feast down to them
which they scoffed with silent enthusiasm, each
thanking us in turn when they had finished. Very
formal, very polite. An even smaller kid came in
as they left and he finished off the soup in the
pan. I don't think he dared ask for more and
though we shoved other stuff his way, he shook
his head, thanked us and went back to trying to
sell plastic trinkets.

12 January

John is ill this morning. He was running to the
bathroom all night, and looks tired out.

We filmed in the streets again today – me
walking the city looking for Mo's house with his
address in my pocket. We were adopted by a
mangy dog, which followed us. Each time we
stopped it sat in the shade of the van, guarding
the camera gear. The poor mutt needed a square
meal. I walked up and down hills. Passed a man
in a van selling bananas. He was driving in circles
with a loudhailer on his roof out of which came
this babbling, incomprehensible sound,
punctuated every now and again by 'bananas'.
At the same time three officers in uniform
walked down the hill opposite, looking into the
gutters, turning over stuff with their shoes. The
gutters are grim. Anything could be in them.
They spill over the roads, grey water gathering
into a stinking river full of rags and bags,

and presumably whatever the officers were looking for.

Mo was in. He had a parrot that sat on the table eating starfruit and a small dog that wore knickers. He's obviously crazy and I'm going to get on with him too. He has catchphrases like 'A real man should never let the sun come through his legs'. What does that mean? I have no idea. Now we are on board he has a captain's hat on, and a blazer over a Hawaiian shirt. He grew up on these rivers. He's been telling me the same stuff about how hard the *tucunaré* will be to find, that the high water has sent them all off into the undergrowth. I'm getting used to hearing that. I asked him about the Coboclos, the river people we are going to find. They are mixed race. They live in villages by the water and make a living from what the river gives them. They'll have secret places they go fishing.

Arrived at Nova Canaã after dark. The village stands out as a strip of pools of light. But the moon is full and bright enough to bathe the river in a milky blue light, and the clouds are frayed like a moth-eaten scarf. It's a wonderful evening, and great to be out here at last. I'm missing you all. Patrick and Iona would love travelling on this boat. They'd have a bunk bed cabin with their own porthole.

*   *   *

Nova Canaã, 13 January

In bed half asleep. I was woken by a bang on the deck above me. The water pipes of the boat's heating system are gurgling somewhere near my head. The noise comes in waves – fussing, burbling, fizzing away like I'm stuck inside a whale listening to its rumbling digestive system.

The river is much narrower here. Within a few yards of me a green wall of forest stops abruptly, sort of expressionlessly, but the water runs into it, deep under the dark green canopy.

We set off early with Ivandre and Raymondo – two fishermen from Nova Canaã. I try to visualise a river and dry banks when all I can see is water and the upper parts of trees. An hour later we're into a meandering passage through the impassive forest. We're fishing our way upriver, Mo with more catchphrases, like 'I am not fishing I am just stretching the line', or 'Right in front of the fish's mouth' when he puts in a particularly good cast. His captain's hat never leaves his head. I get a follow from a small fish. That's all. We catch nothing. Mo whistles and punches his lures bravely into gaps in the undergrowth, but he doesn't think we'll catch anything either.

My heart sinks but I suppose the story is evolving. We are moving upriver asking questions as we go. At Kambeba, the next village, we will ask other Coboclos if they know where I can find the *tucunaré*. They will say that they do not, but that if I find someone called Raphael, he will know. Raphael is the old man of the river. The man who knows where the secret clear-water lagoons are. Maybe it's good that I haven't caught one. Good for the programme. It's just that I'm doubting I ever will. I'm not sure where the story goes or what we'll do if I don't make it happen.

This conversation went more or less according to script when we arrived at Kambeba. I had to wait on the boat while the villagers were told what to do, and when I came ashore they moved in formation like a welcoming party for a minor dignitary. They relaxed after a bit and smiled and laughed. Later, I walked around their village and sat in the school room learning Portuguese with the kids. I've bought Patrick a great bow and arrow from the son of the chief. For Iona I've found a great necklace made with nuts from the forest.

Got attacked by wasps this evening. We'd gone out to catch piranhas. We stopped the boat by some reeds. I heard shouts and scrambling. Above the prow a swirl of black smoke wreathed the two kids who'd come with us. They waved at the air and jumped head first into the piranha-infested river. Ivano followed them from the other boat. I turned to run, but the boat moved under me like I was going the wrong way on an electric walkway. Mo yanked at the starter cord. The engine spluttered. I heard buzzing. I jumped: an inelegant arse-first bomb into the river. Three or four feet under, time slowed and I remembered two things: first, my sunglasses had been on my head and weren't any more; second, I was wearing one of Miles's really expensive microphones. My hand found my sunglasses as I reached for the surface, but when I came up Miles looked sick. I tried to explain that I was sorry. Miles shook his head and said, 'It's f*&@*d. It's just f*&@*d. It's f*&@*d,' over and over.

14 January

We moved last night and woke in a Led Zeppelin mist. I've no idea how far we've come, though I loved drifting in and out of sleep as the boat moved upriver, feeling it heave sideways around the tight meanders. The sky stayed clear, the moon bright, and every so often I leant down off my bunk and craned a look through my porthole to see the silvery forest closing in as we ascended the narrowing river. This morning feels good.

We found Raphael, the old man who knows where the bass and the secret lagoons are. He is short, wiry, with a friendly, enquiring face. I can tell straight away, despite our faltering, translated chat, that he's a real angler, that he understands fish and fishing. We talk of our chances, of weather and water levels. Of course he explains that the water is high and that the fish are in the trees. I ask about the lagoons. He does know of some, but he hasn't been to them for a while. Still, he agrees to take us there.

We motored upriver, Mo and Raphael chatting busily. But when we found it the lagoon was indistinguishable from the spreading expanse of water all around, and it was brown. The day was unravelling fast, but this is when it is all supposed to happen.

I cast and cast but without any real conviction that I'll ever meet with a bass. The water stretches for ever, deep into the forest. I know the fish are in there, way beyond reach. Finally, Mo tells me to reel in. We've given up on the lagoon. I ask if there are others. Mo says maybe. And on we went. We didn't stir a fish. Mo threw his lure with unflagging enthusiasm. 'I just stretch the line. Oh did you see that cast? That was brilliant! In front of the fish's mouth.' I didn't see the point: we'd come to the wrong place at the wrong time, and the flood would take weeks to subside. The film was screwed.

Suddenly Mo was wrestling with his rod, cranking the reel handle like he was winching a boat up on to a trailer. 'Yes. Twenty kilos. Twenty-five kilos!' I thought he was kidding until a bass leapt through the surface, fell and bounced off it two or three times, jangling the tip of Mo's rod up and down. A bass! We'd found a bloody bass!

Mo caught another soon after and then two came in attached to the same lure. Mo whimpered with excitement. 'I can't believe it!' he said. 'Can you see? Two at once. I think I'm gonna have an orgasm right here.' I caught one too. I switched to my fly rod and caught a hatful. We had a basket of small bass to feed the village where we had been staying. We came back and cooked them with the girls. And with a plate of bass and rice on my lap, and with the village kids on the sand at my feet, the firelight dancing across my face, I tried to do my piece to camera which will end the whole film. God, it was difficult. I said the right things. I was speaking from the heart. I believed every word I said. But I'm not sure I sounded as though I did. We did three or four takes. My food went cold. The kids got bored and shuffled off and had to be brought back in again. Sometimes maybe I just think too damn much.

15 January-ish – it's hard to tell now

Manaus again. Now we're trying to film the first half of the story. On the way back from Kambeba Ivano found a lodge – some place where he used to work – that can fit us in. They say they are catching fish. So we won't have to fly home only to turn round again. A shame: I'd been hatching a plan to drive up to Venezuela to chase bonefish for a few days instead!

It is Sunday. There are impromptu parties all

over the place, flatbed trucks full of speakers, kids playing football in side streets, and in the middle of the city hundreds of people flying kites – the kites in dog fights, swirling and diving against a clear blue sky. It looks great.

After a lot of driving we found the sort of street carnival John was looking for. Twenty or thirty musicians beating out a tune. I got into the middle of the crowd. The others found a balcony to film from. Fireworks and bangers streak into the air. The band went quiet for a moment, then a new tune began. A six-foot, raven-haired Amazonian stepped in front of the band, held her hands high in the air – five o'clock shadow under each arm – paused, then caught the beat and everything started at once – belly, hips, arms and legs in a frenzied, four-way rhythmical wiggle. Halfway through her dance I noticed Ivano scuttling round behind the band, deep in negotiation. Nathan had appeared beside me training the camera from me to the Amazonian and back again. Miles was grinning knowingly. Oh shit. I'm going to have to dance with her. She pulled me across the road. It's impossible. I'm sober, a gazillion people are watching, and I could only ever dance to The Jam anyway. Eventually I shake my arse and point a little. But the Amazonian is on her own again, back with the crowd, fuelling wet dreams. I'm left beside her boogieing really badly, wondering what the hell to do next, when this drunk, bald dwarf joins in with me and my life is over: this is going to be televised for God's sake!

Later – my day really going wrong now – in a misguided attempt to drink enough to dance after the dancing is over, long after there is any chance of me rebuilding the scene that is so painfully crystallised on the tapes Sam is busy logging, I have a few beers too quickly. Ivano – I swear the Devil is never far from that guy's shoulder – mentions that the two ladies sitting on a nearby table would like to join us for a drink. Am I the only one not to spot immediately that they are tarts? I say, sure, if they want a chat, why not? Only being friendly after all. But Katrina wants more. She says I am very handsome and asks if I like women. John and Nathan start an incredibly absorbing conversation. Sam is safely chatting with Ivano, who is giggling like a fiend. Katrina's friend Erica comes over and sits next to Miles, who gives me a kind of 'you got us into this, you get us out of this' look.

'You no likey women?' Katrina coos beside me. She has the look of a well-exercised and suntanned chicken and she's about a million years old. How could I have guessed? She must be the most unemployed tart in Brazil. I say, yes, I do like women, in fact I am married to one. I show her my ring. 'Ah! *Esposa*.' Yes, that's right. *Esposa*. 'Is OK. In Amazonia everyone is free. I want to give you all-over massage.' Her hand lands on my thigh. I remove it. 'Where is your hotel?' It lands back there again. She's like shit on a blanket. I show her pictures of the kids. Then of you. At this point her resolve weakens. '*Esposa*,' she says. 'She is very pretty.' Yes. That's right. Very pretty.

That snake Ivano laughs all the way to the pizza bar, while Sam looks at me like I'm mad.

We're flying back to the start of the story tomorrow, to the lodge that will give us awesome fishing and five-star comfort, but an incomplete sense of the country. I still want to catch a monster bass, the rip-snorting rod breaker that captured my imagination, and this is the place to do it. Partly for the film I guess, but partly because it's difficult to think about flying halfway round the world to catch a pot full of stuff no bigger than a perch. In that sense I can't wait to get in a few hours of proper fishing. But I know, I just know the place will be full of fat Texans with worming rods.

18 January

We've been to the lodge. We didn't catch anything, so now we are back in the Mystery Machine going at light speed to a dam north of Manaus called Balbina. It is the one place in Brazil where the water levels will not have been screwed by this apocalyptic rain. A few minutes ago we drove through a town above which

loomed the most enormous plastic statue of the
Virgin Mary. As we passed it we came within
range of a mobile transmitter and all our phones
beeped one after the other as messages came in
from home – a twenty-first-century miracle.

Uvavu is driving like a crazy man. The engine
has no power, but the road is rolling up and
down like the swell of a mega tsunami and on
the downhill sections we are getting up to speeds
the van was never built to cope with – we are
surfing.

I said the lodge would be full of Texans with
burnt foreheads and it was. The dining room was
like Brobdingnag – enormous chairs and tables
hewn from rainforest hardwood and at them
enormous Americans. I watched one of them
drink a pint of Coke for breakfast! Lots of syrup,
lots of bacon. Fat arses in safari shorts.
Overstressed knees. Swollen trainers. God, it was
like Bruegel had kitted out one of his scenes from
a Columbia catalogue.

But I have to admit the most charming person
in the place was Tim – a very, very big truck
salesman from Georgia. He invited me to join him
in his boat and when the rain came down like
God was draining the bath, it was Tim who took
it best. He was happy to stay out, happy to come
in. We should have stayed out of course but we
were soaked through. Danny, our monosyllabic
guide, drove us into the rainstorm at forty knots

before we had put our coats on. John wanted the crew to dry out.

We came in. We dried off. And later in the day we went back out again. I finally convinced Danny that we had to fish against the hard banks, the places where the river was confined, not in the forest. We found an earth cliff and a couple of streams running out of it, making little coves off the main flow. When the first bass hit I couldn't help shouting out some very post-watershed commentary. But it was tiny. Another hit a minute later and though it felt bigger this one came off. I tried and tried the same spot, but it never showed again. We moved and then I caught the smallest bass in the Amazon basin. I could have wept. But it was such a pretty fish. I love their sulky mouths and all the finery and spikiness of their cloth. I slipped it back and Danny called time. We had hours of daylight left! Hours. But the romper-room rules bring boats off the river at a prescribed time that Danny was only too pleased to conform to.

Later, over a beer at the bar with a few of the Confederate guests I found out they'd caught a couple of enormous bass – seventeen and nineteen pounds. I asked them when. They said both fish hit during the rainstorm.

Had to finish the day with a piece to camera down at the dock. From the point of view of the story, I was making a surprise decision to move

on – because I wanted to see the real Brazil for
myself. Of course I was talking about going
off in search of something we had already been to.
But still I found it one of the easiest pieces I've
done. I think because I was speaking from the
heart. I really would have wanted to move on
for those reasons. I just can't take that Butlin's
fishing – summoned by bells. It does my
head in.

Now we are heading to Balbina dam with no
idea of how it will fit into the story and I couldn't
be happier. It is our last resort for a giant
tucunaré – Ivano remembered it while we were at
the lodge, and said if we hurried we could fish it
for a few hours before our flight home.

The drivetrain is whirring wildly at maximum
revs. At the trough of each swell the road is
generally broken and potholed. We brake hard
and slalom wildly past the holes. And strangely,
this mad dash is making sense of everything. I'd
love to go back and do that closing piece to
camera at Kambeba again. I really did need the
context. I said how I was glad to have left the
lodge, to have gone in search of the real Brazil,
that I had set myself the simple goal of following
the fishing rod wherever it would take me, that I
had had the most amazing adventure. I knew all
of that was true, but I hadn't felt it yet. Now I
wouldn't change a word, but I know it would be
different.

I don't care about the big bass any more. The film doesn't need it. I don't need it.

The dam was a wasteland anyway, full of dead trees, sticking up out of the water like thousands of stalagmites, bleached white in the sun. We could have run our little canoe with its crazy, sewing-machine outboard for days on end and never reached the far limits of the place. My guide, a kid in a van Nistelrooy strip, hurriedly grabbed off the street and put in charge of the canoe by the guy who hired them out, was fantastically clueless. He kept stalling the engine, he ran us into several trees and he had no idea where the fish were.

I fished hard: casting, stripping, casting, stripping, willing the scaly bastards to show up with an appetite. The place looked like it ought to hold monster fish among all the dead wood and lily pads. At any moment a bloody great bass was going to eat its way into the boat. But I fished for hours for only one pugnacious little bass. It would have been better with nothing. But the Amazon had only small bass to give me and it gave me one more. Our last shot for a monster had failed.

And I loved every desperate, disastrous moment of the effort.

We're heading to the airport now so . . .

N.O.R.W.I.C.H.

Suburban Sea Trout

IT IS DARK ALREADY. HEADLIGHT BEAMS FROM passing traffic swing across me as I fumble with the lock. A police siren wails somewhere on the housing estate to the east. As a background rumble, deeper and softer than the noises of the city that bounce off the yellow sky, I hear the underground sound of water. The River Itchen pours under the road beneath me.

I have dreams like this. Urban escape dreams flying over a municipal pond or a stream in a park. The water drains to reveal hundreds of gigantic, fantastic fish writhing in the mud. I recently rescued an enormous sea trout from a boating pond, and took flight with it from a high building. The fish flew with me, until we reached open countryside, when we dropped like torpedoes into a river and I woke up.

Sea-trout time passed me by completely this year. Normally I try to get over to western Wales at least once in July or August. Or I'll hunt around some of the creeks and inlets near where I live, and turn up a fish or two. They define a summer somehow. I catch so few that my memories of each fish are anchored to places and times, so that eventually sea trout meter out the passing of the years in a way that makes them all the more significant. So it was with a tinge of disappointment that I remembered in October that I hadn't even tried for one. Most sea trout have done their running by then, and I was pretty much out of opportunities to give 2003 a sea-trout memory. I know there are late fish in places like South Uist, but I was stuck at home and couldn't afford much time away. I was moaning about this predicament to William when he suggested I drive down to Southampton that Thursday night.

'Are the Woodmill fish still running?' I asked.

He said that there were fresh fish coming in all the time. One of his friends had cancelled, and now William had the pool to himself and another friend of his called Nick. I was welcome to join them. I had heard enough about Woodmill not to give it a second thought. The upstream limit of the tide running into the Itchen is a circular pool in the middle of Southampton. It may be at the grunge end of the sea-trout spectrum, but it holds big fish.

William's directions get me as far as the exit off the motorway. I turn right and head south, reach a complicated junction without the sign it's supposed to have – and suddenly I'm lost in Southampton's suburban jungle. I'm driving past a bus stop, a betting shop, sex shop, off-licence, chippy, and pub. At the pub I decide I'm going wrong, and turn round to ask at a garage. The spotty kid has never heard of Woodmill. I drive back to the motorway, try again and turn round at the same pub. Finally I give up on the way I'm supposed to be going and navigate by instinct, rolling downhill on the basis that there will be a river at the bottom of it. When I find Woodmill Lane I'm coming from the wrong direction. In the distance is the block of flats William mentioned. I turn left over a bridge, and find myself in front of barred iron gates wondering how I got there.

As I wait for William in the car park, eating a garage sandwich for supper, I hear a splash like someone's dropped a minibar out of the back of one of the planes coming in to Southampton airport. When William arrives I mention that there's a fish in the pool the size of Moby Dick. 'Is there?' he asks casually.

We chat for a while, and set up our rods under the light in the car park. We've got about four hours of flowing tide. William thinks the rising water is OK, but that things will go quiet at full tide, when the pool slackens and it is difficult to find or work the fly through moving water. It's worth starting soon. I've no idea what to tie on – instinctively I feel that the subtlety of a small goat's toe, with its fluttering tendrils of peacock herl, will be lost on these urban fish. William says they'll snap at anything. Then later he lets on he mostly uses a snakefly – a much better name for the setting. I don't have any, but William lends me a couple.

The pool lies inside a perimeter fence, encircled by tall leylandii hedges. A second gate from the lane – sheet metal on a welded frame, with 'Woodmill Pool' in ironwork letters spanning the opening – makes the place look like a prison. The river flows under the road outside and rushes in at the head of a circular pool with concrete edges. A bridge with a metal handrail leads over the inlet to a casting platform in the darkest part of the pool, tucked under a thick hedge. Another casting platform runs a few feet out over the water from under a tall oak, and at the tail of the pool a concrete boat-ramp runs down into the lapping current. I stand there wondering where to start and am struck by the incongruity of the fish and the setting. Light spills out of the car park and the flats opposite, and the street lamps outside, and the whole pool is bathed in a smudgy, yellow glow. Wild sea trout – creatures that have no borders, that are migratory, nomadic – are swimming through this glowing stadium.

A massive sea trout thumps the water under the bushes on the far side, in a part of the pool that looks impossible to cast to. William puts his waders on, and decides to cross to the gravel bank at the lower end of the pool to get an angle across and under the trees. His pal Nick fishes from the stone ramp that runs down on to the water. That leaves me in the dark under the leylandii, or out on the small platform under the oak tree. I try from the bank to begin with, lifting my back cast as high as I can to clear the hedge. A small fish jumps the fly first cast, tussles with it and falls off.

A few sea trout move where the tongue of water running through the middle of the pool starts to curl back, creating an upstream current along my bank. I change angle to reach the most substantial boil, and catch the hedge behind. The fly is stuck hard. It's one of only two of someone else's snakeflies, so I'm reluctant to leave it behind. I find a steel ladder propped against the hedge, and manage to reach a branch of the untamed evergreen, enough to grab hold of as I jump off the ladder. Then I'm stuck in the middle of a sticky, fragrant jungle running my hand up the line, holding the whole tree down under tension, bits of greenery falling down my shirt and itching my head, cursing in the dark, while the sea trout in the pool keep on thumping.

At Woodmill the urgent sounds of a city at night rub away any preconception of what sea-trout fishing ought to be – pitch black, a whisper of water, lilting Welsh accents dripping across a wet meadow. Instead, doors slam, there is shouting, and cars pass with the muffled throb of heavy music. The air has a tang to it, especially when the tide goes out and the waterfall fills the air with a damp thrice-through-human-kidneys mist. It is never dark.

The river flows in from upstream in pulses as the tide slowly rises. Every twenty minutes or so a whirring noise precedes a sudden rush of water. A jet of fast-flowing water pushes right out into the pool. The sea trout respond by crashing around twice as busily, three or four at a time. The biggest always jump over in the dark corner under the trees, and occasionally under my feet where I lean on the handrail as the water rushes. One thumping splash cuts across all of these, confrontational and massive.

'That's the minibar fish again, William.'

'I hear it,' he says. William is just visible as a silhouette against the water.

I have my fly back, but the greenery behind confines me to one angle, across and upstream. On the third or fourth cast the line suddenly draws tight, and I lift the rod, alive to any sign that this might be a big one. But the beating tail sends urgent vibrations up the line and I guess that it's a finnock – a young sea trout. The fish comes splashing to the surface, turns and dives, taking twenty feet of line with it. It's a proper sea trout but a small one for Woodmill – only two or three pounds. I have to climb down a ladder to unhook it – the tide is rising but the water is still four feet down. The ladder runs down the wall of the pool to a line of slippery rocks and weed. My fish flicks off the line as I get to it. It counts, though.

I fish on and catch the hedge again, before trying a few casts from the platform. The night is quieter. It's about twelve, or twelve thirty. The last plane passed overhead an hour ago. Most of the lights in the block of flats have gone out, the police sirens have stopped. A few minutes ago I heard two loud bangs like gunshots, but nothing afterwards. Just the dull hum of a city falling asleep. An owl hoots from the trees behind. The tide is up a bit, and the sea trout are crashing around more than ever, but after a good thumping take, and another splashy pull from a finnock, the fishing has quietened down along with the city. I've heard noises from the far side of the pool where William is, and Nick had one good fish early on, another smaller one since.

William wades ashore before he gets cut off by the tide, and I walk over to ask how he's done. He's caught four. It's time for a coffee. A street light on the bridge creates a circle of reflected light at the end of the main flow. As William tells me about the sea trout he's had this year, including one an ounce under ten pounds and the night they caught over twenty, I watch for fish. One good sea trout has moved three times in the same spot. William explains that Woodmill is over a thousand years old, and was built for netting salmon. The fish must have run under the bridge, into an oval pool with one upstream exit. They would have stacked up in here in their thousands. Netting them was easy slaughter. Now there is no netting and there are not many salmon.

* * *

It's a clear October sky, and the air has cooled quickly over the water. A thin mist is visible where the light comes through the bridge, a narrower band of light now the tide is up. We think there might be another half-hour or so till high tide when the fishing will drop dead. William starts again under the glow of the street light at the head of the pool, trying the near channel where a huge fish was caught a few weeks back. I try the casting platform again to cover the spot where I have seen that fish move. I pull back quickly on the line to stop the fly washing back towards me and a fish hits at the end of one long draw.

It's a heavy thump. The line stops solid and then as I tighten I feel a stubborn headshake. The sea trout stays deep for only a few seconds then rushes up and through the surface, convulsing across the top. With the line back on the reel, I edge back off the platform and along the bank towards William and his net.

'Got one?' he asks nonchalantly.

'Yes. It's a good fish.' It seems I'm far more excited than I ought to be. But the trout suddenly pulls line and dives. I can't help myself.

'Er . . . It's a good fish. I think I'll need your net.'

William is reluctant to stop fishing to help me land a fish he deems to be totally ordinary.

'Yes . . . Well, you are playing it like a complete fairy.'

'It's a good fish. It feels heavy.' I pull it in harder, turning it up through the water. Responding to the pressure the trout jumps clear in front of us.

'OK. It's not bad.'

Finally William puts his rod down. We get the net under the trout and heave it on to the wet grass. I dig around for my torch. It's a fat hen, peppered with tiny black spots across a background of tarnished silver — the colour just starting to turn. The hook comes out easily, and I decide to put it back. At the bottom of the stone jetty I fan water across its gills, feeling the body harden, the tail start to beat. After a minute the trout swims out of my grasp back into the pool.

'Six pounds,' concedes William. 'A good fish.'

Suddenly I feel the cold, and how tired I am. It's two o'clock. The fish are still jumping occasionally, but the tide is slack now, and the pool feels subdued. The night has changed. I have my 2003 memory. It is time to pack in.

Breakfast in Bhutan: A Notebook

FIRST DAY IN BHUTAN: THE AUSTRIAN CARPET-SELLER homed in like a hungry bear on the five of us as soon as we sat down. Oh dear! He was wearing a gho with taut black socks, knees and thighs bulging white above them, a sweaty forehead, and eyes half hidden behind his glasses. He talked remorselessly about his carpet collection, his singing-bowls, and his biking exploits. He offered to show us his carpet shrine, and most bizarrely his swinging chair – pronounced 'schvingging'. For some reason, Nathan said he'd be keen to see it. Anyway, he invited himself to dinner like he'd invited himself to drinks, and we listened with dying enthusiasm to his ambition to build an Austrian village in the Himalayas, and to more un-hilarious motorbiking japes. Then he outlined part of the bowl therapy he'd perfected. It involved sitting with your feet in a singing-bowl of water while he performed two hours of inquisitive psychoanalysis to reveal blocked chakras and general personality disorders, and it occurred to me that it was me or him

– one of us was clearly very disordered. I could see John framing sequences in his mind, but if John thinks he's filming the swinging Attila unblocking my chakras he's got another think coming!

I come back to my room each night to find everything has been very neatly prepared – bed turned down, towels arranged, lights on dim – and the door to the TV cabinet has been left open. A vast Samsung A2 Nicam stereo. I refuse to see what is on it, but guess they must be very proud of their television.

Chatting with me and Ugyen over breakfast, Kuenzang jokes that he doesn't sin: 'No drink, no smoke.'

Ugyen says: 'Only betel nut and girls.'

'No,' sighs Kuenzang. 'That chapter is closed. Now when I tease the girls they call me uncle.'

Sunday. On the way to the festival at Paro Dzong, I was talking to Ugyen. Bhutan is changing. The roads make travelling around the place different now. The rugged terrain kept communities apart – that's why it's such a diverse country. Ugyen's parents keep telling him how lucky he is: they had to trek for days from Bhumtang carrying only a few light clothes and some food. There's much more meat in the diet than there used to be. Thirty years ago people ate meat only once a year. And the litter – all the plastic is new; the Bhutanese haven't worked out how to deal with it yet.

I asked about the big knobs painted on all the houses. We needed to explain this to camera, because they are so obvious. Ugyen told me about the Divine Mad Monk, Lama Drukpa Kunley. The lama used his penis to subdue evil spirits, so now penises are painted on the walls of houses to ward them away.

We ate lunch in Paro, laughing more and more about our favourite 'dreadfully high' joke and now the schvingging-chair and singing-balls – then drove to Thimpu, listening to 'Feeling Good' on the way up. The crew stopped to film some kids, but the kids ran away.

We found the karaoke bar this evening. It is down a side street, past some shops selling fruit and vegetables, lit brightly, a burst of scent and colour in an otherwise grey and smelly alleyway. A few teenagers mill about at the foot of a stairwell. The stairwell is dark and fetid. Inside is a bandstand in one corner, a bar in the other, a clear area of floor. A young man is crooning into the microphone; behind him a keyboard player, guitarist and someone on an electric drum kit. Most of the kids in there are sitting down and watching – well behaved and relatively animated by the show. At the back a few of the lads are getting rowdy, shouting 'All right' and 'Shake it, baby!' We are asked if we'd like to have someone sing or tape-dance. That's how it works here – someone comes round with a book and you pay 50 ngultrum for a song, or 100 ngultrum for a tape-dance, then you get to nominate the dance, song and singer. When a pretty girl gets up to sing the lads at the back shout and heckle her, but the place still feels surprisingly timid and respectful given the age of the drinkers. Two big red phalluses hang from the doorway. I get a Tiger beer and sit down to watch.

Night in Thimpu was full of dogs again. My earplugs were uncomfortable, so when I woke up at three and all was quiet I took them out. Ten minutes later the first dog started. One muffled bark or growl led quickly to a storm of howling and barking across the city, then it all died down again. At one point a cat began to mew plaintively – until by the sound of it she was either treed or ripped to bits. Karma said it was the 'music of Bhutan', which is a nice way of viewing howling packs of dogs.

None of us slept well. John was woken first by the dogs, then by Miles turning on the light looking for earplugs, then later by Miles leaping about with a dead arm. Breakfast was awful: grey, gruel-like porridge which tasted bitter and empty. The toast was weird, the milk strange. A symptom perhaps of the increase in tourism – the Bhutanese feel they need to cater for Western tourists. Seven years ago the choice was boiled eggs and coffee, and breakfast was better for all that.

Today was my meeting with the Director-General of

Tourism. Formality is so very important here. He is very smartly turned out, even wearing a ceremonial sword. I see he has notes on his desk about his meeting with the BBC, about the philosophy of Bhutan, about travelling in a spirit of peace, about the development of the country – two pages of carefully ordered thoughts which he wants to convey to us. But in the event the bright camera light makes him blink terribly and he is so nervous he can hardly speak. I try to fill in most of the gaps for him, and accept my fishing permit in what I hope is the correct manner. I tell him how grateful I am for permission to fish in his lovely country.

At Dochu La, there are prayer flags everywhere. Ugyen tells me a little about the significance of mountain passes – as windy spots. The prayers on the flags blow away on the breeze. The prayers are for all creatures, as Buddhists believe that all creatures 'are our mothers', and it is the intent of Buddhists to carry the whole of creation with them on their spiritual journey. I am looking across at the cumulus shrouding the Punakha valley. Up here in the clouds it's serene, peaceful, even other-worldly.

We arrive in Gangte after a gruelling three-hour drive from Talo and Nubang, most of it in the dark. Perhaps it's for the best. There's a precipitous slope inches away from the wheels of our truck and Tashi's getting increasingly sleepy. An hour after dark he begins to nod and yawn, and holds third gear out of crawlingly slow corners, chuntering the engine at 800 rpm under full load, absolutely killing the crankshaft and bearings. I ask if he is OK and in the end he makes it, waking up and putting his foot down.

The track into the village bounces and jars through ruts and puddles, snaking between hand-cut wooden fences and timber barns. To my left in the dark chasm of the valley lies the river I have come halfway across the world to see again – the sacred Gangte Chhu, a spring-fed stream in the Himalayas, my fly-fishing Shangri-La.

I feel uplifted, as though we have entered a different Bhutan. But the same thoughts strike me as last time: how tourism is a form of erosion – for a little to be experienced a little must be worn away. I feel that even more keenly now, because there are more hotels, more Western breakfasts. And what's to blame? TV! What an unbelievable irony! What a hypocrite!

The guest house is just as I remembered, plus a few light bulbs which may be here for our benefit. A big fire is burning outside. We have tea out of a flask as we arrive, followed by the best meal we have eaten so far: rice, okra, fiddlehead ferns, chilli and cheese curry. The food is all perfectly done, served to us in the open air as we sit around the fire. When I am full, I lean back and see the moon drifting through vaporous clouds, and I feel like barking, just like the dogs.

* * *

In the morning we explore the village. At dawn it is ridiculously picturesque. The sky is a high blue, the sun – not yet over the hills – cuts an angle of filtered light across the shadowed slopes. Smoke comes from each chimney. Cows wander about the road and on to people's porches. A pair of dogs wrestle and snarl. We are filming beside a house when out comes a little girl in a small gho and pink wellies with a tooth-brush, followed by her mum and dad, also brushing their teeth. The little girl looks at us, mesmerised by the camera. Her brother and sister appear next, each carrying a bag of crisps. The little girl starts to cry – she wants one. Her sister runs over and plants a crisp in her mouth. Then another kid appears from the neighbouring house in a *101 Dalmatians* T-shirt. I show them my camera, take pictures of them, then show them the pictures. They push each other out of the way to be in a picture. Another boy joins in. He pulls a ridiculous face when his mouth is full of crisps – they all find the result side-splittingly funny.

We wander through the village, Nathan taking shots of families washing, kids getting ready for school, kittens playing. At one of the houses, Ugyen arranges for us to have tea. All the family is there – Grandma, Mum and Dad, three kids, the eldest a girl of fourteen who has a tiny amount of English. They make me a cup of tea and bring out a carpet for me to sit on, and I settle myself next to them to do a piece to camera about the village and my day ahead. The littlest girl has a cough. Her big sister tells me there are 546 children in her school and 18 teachers.

A small boy comes running up to me as we leave the village. He hands me a piece of paper with his name on. He is looking very smart in his gho, ready for school, but I think I must have taken a picture of him earlier, that he was the kid in the *Dalmatians* T-shirt and assume he wants me to post it to him. I take another very formal portrait of him standing by a pile of logs and say I'll send it to him. I MUST NOT FORGET!

The Gangte landscape is softer than any other in Bhutan. Even the surrounding peaks are rounded, falling down tree-lined ridges then slumping into grass slopes, which ease into a softer-falling plain of spongy moss, rhododendron and dwarf bamboo. The river has cut a sinuous meander through all this, turning in on itself over and over. Rivulets seep through the hillocks of bamboo. Stands of dark, peat-stained water, floating mats of grass. The slopes fall in stages, like a dumped pile of sand, softening in gradient. Even so, there is little flat ground – only that inside the passage of the mazy river. The head of the valley is split by a spur; two streams meet immediately above where the road crosses the valley. Somewhere in the forested slopes above, these streams break from underground – it is impossible to say which is the principal one.

The fishing in the Gangte is as brilliant as I

remember. It is the perfect trout stream, completely unspoilt, sheltered in that buffer of marshy ground. I catch fish after fish, all small but all on a dry fly. They are so free-rising and so pretty! In one pool I get a surprise. A trout as big as a U-boat. It is at least two feet long – it looks like it's landed from outer space. I try to catch it for over an hour. Only when a small fish takes my fly does the big fish move – it turns and chases the hooked trout across the pool and eats it off the line.

It is a strange thought, that this perfect river flowed for so many thousands of years with no trout in it.

Sam got really ill here. He lay in his room, white and groaning, and missed everything. We thought we might have to leave him behind.

Driving through the pass between Trongsa and Bhumtang we climb from 6,000 to 11,000 feet in forty minutes. Water bottles and ears pop. The prayer flags rattle in a stiff breeze – or rather they crackle, with the sound of fire ripping dry brush.

Chendebji Chorten and the black mountains are the backdrop now. In front of them trees drip beards of moss and blur the horizon. Wispy, smoking white clouds peel off the ridge, spiralling in the wind.

Ugyen has his tin can, line and spinner hidden in his gho. We finish our conversation for the camera and leap down the slope, enjoying the stolen minutes of freedom from filming. Kuenzang joins us. Ugyen catches a small trout, but we all expected more from such a perfect pool. Ugyen pulls his line in; the place has been overfished.

At Bhumtang I am offered cold white toast when I come in for breakfast. The three pots of jam are the exact three colours of a traffic light. There are bowls of cornflakes in warmed long-life milk. Meanwhile pans are steaming and frying in the kitchen – a big wok is full of fried rice and vegetables. When it looks as though I might not bother with anything but tea, Ugyen offers me some rice – the guides' breakfast. I have a plateful. So do John, Nathan and Miles. Sam is still too croaky to eat much.

It's Thursday. Today I'll finally get to fish on the Tang Chhu. We need to film me on a motorbike first thing. We wake at six, have traffic-light breakfast at six thirty, are away by seven thirty. Miles and I fool around in front of the lodge for a while on the Yamaha Enticer. It's a sort of *Easy Rider* bike – but with only a 100 cc four-stroke it is totally gutless. It has no brakes whatsoever. I write LOVE / HATE across each set of knuckles, rev the engine, and pull in the clutch for the camera. Then I follow the truck, John and Nathan in the back filming. Ugyen is concerned because I am not wearing a helmet, and we may bump into police.

The bike is a shocker, but it's fun to be riding again, and very quickly I feel like swinging it through a few bends. I ride up and down the road for the camera.

We film the dirt track by the river, heading up past a school. A few kids stare at me, wondering what I'm doing buzzing up and down the road, apparently talking to myself.

Nathan spots a suspension bridge. He reckons it would be a good idea if I rode across. It's a stupid idea. This is a pedestrian bridge. A few minutes later I see someone else ride across it. Nathan notices too – so I have to give it a go. It's hard enough getting the bike to the bridge, down a steep, rutted track, around an overhanging boulder. My first time over is terrifying. The bridge is not much wider than the bike, and wobbly, and I make the mistake of looking at the edges, not the end. I feel I'm going to slide into the wire-mesh sides and slice my knuckles open – but I make it to the far side. The return run is much better – I keep my eye on the end of the bridge and go for it. Once on the far side I need to trial-ride the rock path. The rear tyre is bald, but I keep the revs up and make it without falling off. Finally I park the bike by the river for John to film it and with a few minutes free I go to look off the rocks at the tail of the pool. The place is familiar. I think we found it last time when there was a funeral upstream. The river was swollen and the trout wouldn't eat a damn thing. Ugyen confirms that it is a sacred place. When I spot three big fish at the fall-out of the pool and ask if I can have a go, Ugyen says that the place is too sacred, and that I would upset people.

* * *

Breakfast in Bhutan

We drive upriver to launch our butter lamps at the burning lake. The legend is that some dude lit a butter lamp at this spot, swam under the pool and found treasure, and when he resurfaced the lamp was still alight. We launch three in the end, dedicating one to the crew and safe travel, one to all sentient beings and one to good fishing. The final lamp – for fishing – floats right down the pool, alight to the moment it reaches the fall of smooth water into the rapid. Ugyen says that this is very auspicious, that we will have good fishing as a result.

We begin fishing the Tang at the pool behind the warden's hut. Ugyen said it was a good spot – it may even be the pool where I caught my big fish last time – but it is not what I am looking for. Deep and turbulent, it will hold fish, but I need somewhere where they will be taking off the top. I catch one acrobatic pounder with the camera not yet running, and miss another, before pulling in and going in search of my trout run. We drive up the valley. I'm looking for a spot I found last time. I hope I will recognise it. Tashi nearly stops for lunch, but I insist we keep on, passing familiar places – the temple under the overhanging rock; the pools on the corner where Patrick was stoned; the deep section where I dropped my camera – until finally I see what I think must be the place. We can't afford to skip up the stream taking chances. Hoping I can trust my memory, I commit. We all get out and trudge over.

When I am close, I despair that I'm wrong, that it is too shallow. But this is the spot. I catch fish after fish, all on camera, ending with one really big hen trout from the best lie in the pool, the lie I'd been wading to, talking about covering the whole way down the run. We stop for lunch, the weather whips up and the river dies.

We spend the night at Ugyen's farmhouse. The butter tea ceremony is first. The kitchen is decked out with candles and lamps for atmosphere. Ugyen's white cat is spark out by the stove. Ugyen's dad, Palden, comes in and is asked if he'll sit in the picture. He has a great face, with angular, high cheekbones, a wispy oriental moustache and a beard of just a few straggly hairs. His eyes are watery, his feet bare and hardened, and he is stooped. Ugyen and I talk about the tea. He tells me the cake of tea leaves is a currency, that the older it is the better, the most valuable being a hard, odourless rock. In front of us the boiling tea is poured into a tall wooden churner; lumps of butter and spoons of salt are added; the piston churn is pumped up and down for a couple of minutes, then the brown mix is poured back into a smart, silver teapot. Ugyen's mum pours the boiling mix into the palm of her hand to taste it. A little more salt is added, then she puts her finger to her cheek and twists, as though she is complaining of toothache. In fact, this is a sign that the drink tastes very good.

The five of us sleep in the same room, on a floor

about seven feet by eight feet. It gets cold quickly. Ugyen's dad built the house himself. Ugyen says it is not that good because his dad was architect, carpenter and astrologer – but I think it is superb for one man's work. There are open windows, with sheet-plastic pinned neatly in place for glazing and sliding wooden shutters running in grooves cut into the inner wooden frame. The windows themselves are shaped in the traditional Bhutanese arch. The walls consist of frames hung off solid wooden beams and in-filled whitewashed panels of baked mud. The carpentry around the architrave is decorated with upside-down triangles carved into the angled beam; just above it, the butt ends of the roof-supporting beams are decorated in brick ochre paint within a frame of yellow.

In the centre of the house is a chapel. Ugyen's dad was praying in it when we arrived, chanting in the dark, burning incense, spinning a hand-held prayer wheel. Ugyen's mum and dad are praying in there now as I write at 6.30 a.m. In front of them is the most splendid and ornate carved wooden altar. The altar was designed by Palden, but built by a dedicated carpenter. It is full of statues that Ugyen and his father went to Nepal to get. Nathan comes in to film. John and Miles crowd in behind – Palden does not flinch or cease his prayer. His eyes dart sideways at the camera, but then he continues. Incense is burning; filling the room in a soft, smoky yellow light. The prayer wheel is spinning in Palden's right hand. He is chanting, but never repeating. Later, when it is time to go he appears as if a different person – upright, attentive, bright-eyed. He and his wife seem genuinely delighted to have played host at the last minute to a film crew of five, four drivers and three guides. We thank them, and they say that we are welcome to stay, should we ever come to the Tang again. Since I intend to, I say that I will see them again.

It is the first day of our trek. We will walk from Thimpu to the monastery. Breakfast at the Druk is so terrible it is beyond belief. The tea is grim, the bread stale, the porridge bitter and watery, and festering in tepid pans is a buffet of beans, button mushrooms and slabs of corned beef. I won't eat any of it – out of principle more than anything. Why do they feel they have to interpret Western breakfast for Westerners, instead of just giving us Bhutanese food? I go out to find chocolate in Thimpu, but there is nothing. Obviously I have a face as dark as a cloud because John senses I'm after something, and tries to find out what. I really hate my capacity to get in a self-indulgent sulk, and I'm sure other people must hate it too.

The climb is really hard. I am breathless immediately. We rest. I get breathless again within a few yards. It is compulsory to take it steady, to walk at an even pace that feels unnaturally slow. The breathlessness is rather like swimming underwater, coming up gasping for air, grasping with my lungs, searching for oxygen that isn't there. It is hot in the windless forest. The trail is dusty and steep, winding endlessly, remorselessly upwards, ascending a staircase of tree roots, soil and rocks. The vegetation marks the contours, starting with conifers moving into oaks then rhododendron, juniper and scrub. We will eventually climb above the treeline. Lunch is so welcome. A big cheese roll made with sweet, white bread, prefab cheese and a couple of tomatoes – it tastes brilliant, though the half-boiled spud wrapped in foil is an odd one. The altitude and exercise give me an unbelievable appetite, a chocolate-and-nut craving and a capacity for endless tea and biscuits.

As soon as we reach the clearing by the monastery and the wind whips over the ridge, the temperature drops dramatically. A whirlwind of dust and sticks whizzes past. Three young monks (they are ten years old, but they look about five or six) are playing on the open ground. Beyond the monastery a group of teenage monks is throwing darts at a board. One of them is wearing a Manchester United T-shirt. It gets colder and colder – alarmingly cold, alarmingly quickly. I'm not sure I have enough clothes with me, though I'm sure I'll be fine in the sleeping bag. I daren't look out of the tent to see the dusk drop.

It is morning at the monastery. I am lying in bed, thinking about how the monks must have come up here to be away from people as much as to be closer to God. The landscape of the mountain talks to the soul in a way that closes in on the truth. It's why we find these places so uplifting, so spiritual.

Reaching the stupa at the top of our climb I have a sense of achievement. Those last few hundred metres have been all aching thighs and burning lungs. My head is still pounding, but the view of the Thimpu valley thousands of feet below makes up for it.

The asceticism of the monks has been humbling. Yet in a smaller way the asceticism of this climb seems to make sense of the whole journey – the climb to the lake becoming some kind of spiritual end-point. Certainly a fly-fishing rod takes you to some uplifting places, but this journey has become much more than a fishing trip – it feels like something of a retreat.

We find trout at the lake, trout brought here by a petty crook who was given a clay urn to carry the fish in. They are rising when we arrive and I catch one quickly on a dry fly. But it slips away before I can say anything to the camera and I spend the rest of the afternoon trying to catch another. The place is so quiet. There is no noise. This is their world – a world of complete silence. And now with all the people walking around the lake, the horses being watered, guides hacking at the rhododendron, the trout push off from the sides into the middle and I cannot cast to them. I sit on a rock and wait. Eventually the noise subsides. The trout move back and I get a rise. It is a beautiful fish, yellow underneath darkening to a leather brown with big red spots. From the far shore a slope of rhododendron rises steeply. It is covered in snow and a beard of ice hangs off the rocks at the top. We are so high. These trout are on the roof of the world.

These nights up high pass brokenly, dreaming of suffocation, waking, gasping for air, frost on the inside of the tent and on my sleeping bag, a headache as if an axe were buried in my skull. My sleeping bag feels like a coffin, I can't get comfortable, I go outside for a piss. And out there is a beautiful moonlit night, no sound but the delicate ringing of horse bells.

Silence.

On the trek back it's overwhelming: the sound and beauty of the silence.

Wash and Tope

THERE'S A PUB IN HUNSTANTON BY THE AMUSEMENT arcade, beyond the chippy, called the Wash and Tope. With my back to it I can see right across to Skegness. I like to stand there once in a while licking a double-cone 99, thinking about fifty-pound tope chasing flatties over the sandbanks of the Wash.

The 99 comes after a lost hour in the amusement arcade – somewhere at the age of forty I really ought not to be bothering with any more. When I was ten I wasted days in the arcade on Hunstanton pier, shooting at tin ducks with squiffy air rifles, feeding money into the 'What the Butler Saw' peep show – a selection of saucy postcards peeked at through a keyhole – and the horse-race betting machine. But the pier fell down in a storm and the rest was destroyed in a fire. The tin ducks, and the peep show, are gone too, but somehow the horse-race machine has found its way to another arcade by the pub. I love wasting a few coins in it, though I go less and less often, as the age gap between me and all the real kids in there gets wider. But these intersections with the past are cathartic in a way.

Imagining those giant tope is also an intersection with the past, and it has the same effect, though I had never even seen one until last year. But the fishing stories I read when I was young left strong impressions. By far the most vivid, the one that still plays in my head like the memory of a real event, was by a writer on sea fishing who became obsessed with tope. He described catching his first standing by the boat ramp on a stone jetty, as the tide ripped along the sea wall below and rain fell heavily in the dark. After a long wait the fish took the bait and rushed out to sea, the line unwinding into the darkness. I can see the line glinting under the street light, stretching out across the water, disappearing into the night, rain streaking through a disc of phosphorous yellow thrown from the harbour light. I can hear the reel crackling and the swell knocking against the jetty. He fought this brutal fish for ages without any idea what it was, until finally he dragged it up the sea wall – a massive tope of thirty or forty pounds. I loved the idea that someone could catch a monster like that – a giant dogfish really but shark enough for a child's imagination – within yards of houses, so close to all the nuzzling smells and cosiness of a town fast asleep. The image stayed. I longed to catch a tope, but had no idea where to start. By the time I'd grown old enough to find out I was into other fish, not sea monsters, and the tope remained nothing more than my recollection of someone else's memory.

In fact, the tope that scythed its head to and fro over the damp jetty of my imaginings swam for real within sight of the lookout in the roof of my parents' house. These days, a mazy, silt-choked inlet between the house and the sea still holds a few fishing boats and a row of wooden jettys made from recycled brick pallets and fencing posts. I was standing on one of these a while ago, looking for mullet, when its owner came up and frostily asked me to 'bugger off'. Aesop's way of the wind never being as persuasive as that of the sun, I stuck around. Eventually I got him talking. His name was Brian. I asked about his boat, what he used it for. He took fishing trips, he said, into the Wash after whatever was out there, but particularly tope. I told him that I'd always wanted to catch a tope and asked if there was any chance of joining in on a trip. No, he said, without looking up. He was fully booked for the summer. I asked about cancellations, and about next season. But I'd been standing on Brian's jetty and though I'd disarmed him with talk about fish, he wasn't about to share a boat with me. Finally he said that his son Ben might take me out, if I got a group together. Ben charged 250 quid a day and would take four of us.

It wasn't difficult to find three others. None of us had even seen a tope, but we all fancied what passed for shark fishing in the seaside donkey-ride Wash. I bought boxes of squid from the fishmonger in East Lynn, mackerel feathers from Tower Tackle and dug a few lugworms the night before to catch flatties:

fresh fish – mackerel or flounders – always make the best bait.

The low downs of the north coast cascade to a strip of salt marsh and sand. Driving over the top as the land drops away towards the Wash I feel like I'm surfing down falling waves of a chalk swell. Between the sea and the hills is an uninterrupted dome of sky. Looking down from the hills the coastal strip is broken with dark green eruptions of Scots pine, and feathery rows of poplar. A narrow line rises above the trees and ends at the dark smudge of a barn beside an inlet from the sea.

Paul was waiting by the barn in his Alfa. Big Ben was there too. Henry showed up soon after, dropped off by his girlfriend. We chatted and assembled our kit. We had plenty of stuff, little of it appropriate. What we lacked was any idea of what the hell we were doing. Brian told us we were late and introduced us to his son Ben. He hung about darkly for a while until the pain of watching us nanny around with jokers' kit became too much.

'There's a tide to make,' he said. And he walked off to his professional-looking boat, where four professional-looking anglers sat, impatient to get going.

As Brian's boat moved out into the channel, the engine pitch rising purposefully, Ben turned to watch his father leave. We were supposed to follow him. But a telepathic dawdle overcame us all. Brian was at the end of the harbour channel, heading through the gap in the sandbar, while we diligently arsed about waiting for the rhythmic throb of his engine to die on the wind. A skylark sang in the air above us. We ferried lunch boxes, coats, a bucket of worms, boxes of squid, bags of beer. A tin box rattled with lead weights, swivels, hooks and a knife, a pile of old rods and reels – a boyhood garage collection of stuff not up to the job – appeared on the deck of Ben's fishing boat.

'So, Ben,' I said. 'Any idea where we're going now that we've unfortunately lost touch with your dad?'

Ben said he knew where to go.

Ben's boat was a still-floating version of the many walnut-shaped fishing smacks buried up to their Plimsoll lines and beyond in the mud and samphire of the salt marshes around the harbour. Unlike his dad, Ben did not fish full-time, but this proven if age-worn crate was perfect for trips at weekends. Its fat-bottomed Tudor-warship hull was to do for me later in the day, though.

A gentle swell pushed small waves into the mouth of the channel where it breached the sandbar. The boat bounced briefly, then settled as we made way for a point several miles offshore. The four of us sat on the prow looking back, while Ben steered from the potting-shed cabin. It was the first time in forty years I'd ever looked back at the beach from the sea I'd so often looked out on. And everything seemed smaller.

* * *

Wash and Tope

When a tope picks up the bait it needs to run without dragging the anchored lead across the sea floor: it is best to use a plastic boom so that the line from the reel runs freely through to the hook, and the lead hangs square off the boom. I'd assumed Ben would have the booms and lead. Ben had assumed we knew enough to bring stuff like that with us. At first we improvised using old swivel links, but a good fish took the bait, ran hard and snapped the line. We reckoned the swivel had jammed on the running line. This was going to be a problem. We all searched Ben's boat for the discarded remnants of more organised trips, turning up a few plastic beads and two booms. Ben rummaged around for lead in a tin box behind his engine and after some work – and ingenuity – we had two rods ready for anything.

Soon the wind freshened against the running tide, and a swell picked up. Ben's boat began to roll against the anchor rope. Hefty, roller-coaster sways out of all proportion to the sea beneath us. I was at the bait table cutting strips of mackerel when I looked up to see the mast swinging side to side through sixty degrees. Stupidly I carried on cutting. I was on my knees, intent on what I was doing, with no fixed horizon for a reference point. And I'm a land-lubbing fairy in those easy swells. The smell of fresh fish guts, the rolling boat, the sight of Paul enjoying a bacon sarnie: by the time I decided to leave the bait the game was decided: I had green bile rising fast and my head was pounding. Ben thought I looked pale and asked if

I'd like a cup of tea. I thought it might settle me. I held on to it for ten minutes at most.

We hit a good patch of mackerel straight away, and the lugs stayed in the bucket. While I was chucking up over the side of the boat, Paul, Henry and Big Ben gleefully jigged until the bait bucket was overflowing, and I had to remind them, in between heaves, that we were out here to catch baby sharks, not baby tuna.

It was a long wait. Ben thought there must be too many mackerel around, making easy pickings for tope, and slow sport for us. We drank a lot of tea. We had a lengthy discussion about how quickly a Subaru Impreza will go around a roundabout. Ben got on the mobile in his potting shed to see if anyone on his father's boat had caught a fish. On deck we heard snippets of the chat, including the phrase 'thirty pounds'. This didn't go down well. Paul went back to the mackerel.

I felt better after losing my breakfast. I stared intently at the horizon for half an hour and was rosy enough to join in on the third brew. Ben was lighting the kettle, ducked down in the wheelhouse, when Henry's rod popped out of its hold like a champagne cork, the reel already unloading viciously into the sea. It clattered down the deck towards the stern. Paul shouted, 'Stop that rod,' and Henry ran across to grab it. It slammed against the edge of the boat, jammed momentarily. Henry dived and got the butt of the cork in his hand. The tope kept running.

Henry stood and lifted the rod high in the air to clear the line. At two hundred yards the fish slowed, then picked up again and ran another fifty. We gathered around Henry, and watched the spool of monofilament shrinking.

'What the hell are we going to do if it doesn't stop?' Henry said. 'Can I strike when it's running?'

'Hit it next time he slows,' suggested Ben.

The tope is a scavenger. Its first instinct when it finds an easy meal is to bolt before a bigger tope sees it – like a feral dog with a good bone getting away from the pack. When the run stops the tope is turning the bait ready to swallow. That is the time to strike. The reel paused and Henry struck hard, before the fish ran again and spooled him.

'Is it still there?' Big Ben asked.

'Think so,' said Henry.

The tope was now firmly on the line, but there's a lot of stretch in three hundred yards of nylon, and as Henry winched the beast towards us the dog-with-a-rat headshakes grew steadily more animated. Alongside the boat it thrashed and gnashed according to script.

Ben pulled on a leather glove and leant over the gunwales to grab it by the tail. He swung it aboard. The tope – definitely more small shark than big dogfish – lay grunting on the deck, writhing its head from side to side. We all stepped back and looked for teeth. Two of us tried to pin it down while Ben navigated the jaws to unhook it. The mackerel was still there behind a row of saw-blade gnashers. The tope twisted under us, impossible to hold still, stinking of iodine.

Henry posed for his Big White Hunter shot, and then eased the fish back into the sea.

The afternoon wore on. The swell settled and the tide turned, bringing the boat round on its anchor to face the other way. Paul stayed at the stern happily jigging for more mackerel. Henry drank tea, just happy to be afloat now his machismo card had been stamped.

Only Big Ben and I sat on the bow willing our reels to start spinning. Once in a while the boat shifted on its anchor, and the ratchets clicked. Each click had my fingers twitching like a nervy gunfighter. Each bump on the rod tip was examined for signs of life. Occasionally we'd strike anyway only to reel in a bunch of crabs and a clean backbone. Every fresh mackerel thrown to the crabs like this was one less fillet for tea, and I was starting to see those mackerel as the only reward for the day.

'We really need another tope,' I pleaded. The arcade gods of Sunny Hunny must have been pleased with all those coppers I'd fed their slot machines, because as I said it, Big Ben's rod banged against the side of the boat, and his reel croaked into rusty life.

'How old is that line exactly?' I asked casually, as the skinny spool unloaded towards Skegness.

'Don't know,' said Big Ben. 'Old.'

'And how much is there?'

'Er,' he said glancing at the spool, 'not much.'

Ben came out of the wheelhouse, took one look at the spool and said, 'You're going to have to strike it on the run. He's about to get away with the rod.'

Big Ben hesitated as the line ran down to nothing. With inches to spare, and the tope still going, he leant back hard and struck three times to set the hook. Our last fish was still there.

This electrifying run is the best part about catching a tope. Set the hook and the fish morphs into a deadweight, occasionally animated by further runs, but none as express-train as the first. The fight is like pulling a bath upriver . . . until the white shape lifts out of the blue, the fish at a tangent to the line, and holding stubbornly. Suddenly it's a shark! Its fin cuts the water, and its eyes are as cold as flint.

Paul looked over the side and said, 'We're gonna need a bigger boat.'

It might not be Amity Island, and it might not be a Great White, but a man must tussle with monsters wherever he lives. Out here on the mushy-peas-and-gravy Wash we wrestle overgrown rock salmon in kiss-me-quick hats.

Acknowledgements

Vicky for everything for ever.

Tristan Jones and Beth Coates at Yellow Jersey, without whom this book would not be a book.

Jonathan Young and all at *The Field* magazine, without whom this fishing writer would not be a fishing writer.

Sharon Smith at SSLA, for being really very good at what she does.

Kimberley Littlemore, for having a good idea.

Julian Mercer, for thinking it was a good idea.

John Miller and Anna Gravelle, along with Sam Gibson, Sally Dyas, Duncan Fairs, Robin Shaw, Nathan Ridler, Miles Harris, Sallie Bevan, Liz Nicol, Louise Britton, Emma Conway and Martin

Pailthorpe, for all turning the good idea into reality.

Paul Attfield-Downes, Jim Babb, Marc Bale, Saad Bin Jung and Suhban, George Birkbeck, Rich and the Boogie Team from Blue Crab Quay, Mark Bowler, Ronnie Butler, Simon Cain, Nick Carrick, Cyril, William Daniel, James and Harry Dawes, Vaughan Driessel and Andrew Keil, Moacir Fortes and Ivano Cordeiro, Tony Hayter, Rod Hughes, Tony King, Tony Ling, Patrick Lloyd, Metal Mickey, Ben Pearson, Peter Power and Hakan Stenlund, Richard Slocock, Jonathan Young and Nick Zoll – all for their good company and for good days spent fishing.

Professor Charles Surprisely, for his guitar fly, and Rachel Thorn, for her French again.

'Holy Grayling', 'Metal Guru', 'Suburban Sea Trout' and 'Wash and Tope' first appeared, in different form, in *The Field* magazine. 'The Curse of Shiva' first appeared, in different form, in *Gray's Sporting Journal*. 'My Kingdom Come' first appeared, in different form, in the *Daily Telegraph*. 'Paradise Found' first appeared, in different form, in *Fly Rod and Reel* magazine. All photographs are reproduced by permission of the author.